D1424032

Conscience in World Religions

CANTERBURY BOOKS

General Editor: Robert Hannaford, Professor of Christian Theology in the Bishop Otter Centre for Theology and Ministry at the Chichester Institute of Higher Education.

This series of books explores topics that have a direct bearing upon the development of the Christian tradition of thought. The books will address theological issues directly related to the faith and practice of the Christian community and explore the interpretative significance of Christian theology for modern life and thought. The contributions are drawn from a number of different theological disciplines and schools of thought and should be of interest both to the specialist reader and the educated general public.

Already Published

Peter Davie
Raising Up A Faithful People: High Church Priests and Parochial Education 1850–1910

Robert Hannaford [Editor]
The Future of Anglicanism: Essays on Faith and Order

Robert Hannaford [Editor]
A Church for the Twenty-First Century: Agenda for the Church of England

Robert Hannaford and J'annine Jobling (Editors)
Theology and the Body: Gender, Text and Idealogy

Conscience in World Religions

Edited by

Jayne Hoose

Gracewing.

Notre Dame

First published in 1999
jointly by

Gracewing
2 Southern Avenue
Leominster
Herefordshire
HR6 0QF

University of Notre Dame Press
310 Flanner Hall
Notre Dame
IN 46556
USA

All rights reserved. No part of this publication may be repro-
duced, stored in a retrieval system, or transmitted in any form,
or by any means, electronic, mechanical, photocopying,
recording, or otherwise, without the written permission of the
publisher.

Compilation and editorial material © Jayne Hoose
Copyright for individual chapters resides with the authors.

The right of the editor and contributors to be identified as the
authors of this work has been asserted in accordance with the
Copyright, Designs and Patents Act 1988.

UK ISBN 0 85244 398 6

US ISBN 0268-02353-0
A CIP record for this book has been applied for
and will be available from the Library of Congress

Typesetting by Action Publishing Technology Ltd,
Gloucester, GL1 1SP

Printed in England by
MPG Books Ltd, Bodmin PL31 1EG

291.5

R33953

Contents

Notes on Contributors

Dr George Chryssides is a Senior Lecturer in Religious Studies at the University of Wolverhampton. He read philosophy and theology at the Universities of Glasgow and Oxford, and has published extensively on Buddhism and on New Religious Movements. His book *The Path to Buddhism* was published in 1988.

Helen Costigane studied in Glasgow and London, and lectures in Christian Ethics at Heythrop College, London and the Institute of Ecumenical Studies, Prague. She is writing a doctoral thesis on 'Conscience as the voice of God'.

Dr Ron Geaves is a Lecturer in Religious Studies at the University of Wolverhampton and specializes in Islam and the religions of the Indian subcontinent. He is particularly interested in the transmigration of those faiths to Britain and has published several articles in that area. He is currently working on a book entitled *The Sufis of Britain*.

Jonathan Gorsky is Education Officer of the Council of Christians and Jews (CCJ) and editor of *Common Ground*, the CCJ journal. He has taught at Bristol University and was formerly Education Officer of Yakar, a Jewish cultural centre in northwest London. He has written a number of articles on Christian–Jewish relations.

Jayne Hoose was formerly a Senior Lecturer at Canterbury Christ Church University College, where she taught in the

Department of Geography. She now concentrates her research on business ethics, particularly tourism ethics and developing countries. She has an MA in Christian Ethics from King's College London.

Dr Dave Leal teaches philosophy and moral theology at Regent's Park College, Oxford. His research interests include questions of philosophy and language, and conceptual questions in Christian ethical thought.

Dr Stephen Thomas is a Senior Lecturer in Religious Studies at Canterbury Christ Church University College, where he teaches patristics and philosophical theology. He is the author of *Newman and Heresy*, (Cambridge, 1991), which examines Newman's use of the early Church Fathers. He has also published in the areas of personalist philosophy, postmodernism and Orthodox theology.

Foreword

'Give a little whistle and always let your conscience be your guide'

Were it as simple as Jiminy Cricket might have us believe, there would clearly be no requirement for a book of this nature. In practice, however, the place, use and development of conscience as a moral guide is far from straightforward. Within the Christian tradition, particularly the Protestant and Roman Catholic traditions, conscience has long been a topic of heated debate. This debate has highlighted tensions between the individual and the community and raised questions about the balance between authority, revelation and education in Christian ethical thinking. These tensions arise from the different interpretations and levels of importance accorded to a wide range of authoritative sources within the main Christian traditions: Scripture, divine command, early writers, present-day theologians and philosophers, the experience of individuals and the church community, and, in the case of the Roman Catholic Church, the official teaching office of the magisterium. These questions are clearly in evidence in the first part of this volume, which provides an insight into a range of Christian perspectives on conscience.

The first four contributions highlight the key features of the ongoing debate about conscience within the Christian tradition and are offered as a constructive contribution to the academic debate within theological ethics. Helen Costigane sets out the historical groundwork in the first chapter, identifying the origins of the western idea of conscience in Greek thinking, the biblical tradition, and the approach of some classical Christian writers. Dave Leal and Jayne Hoose follow this with analyses of the Protestant and Roman Catholic approaches to conscience. Both of these traditions have a long history of debate in this area and neither author would, therefore, claim to cover all viewpoints within the respective traditions. Stephen Thomas writes from an Orthodox viewpoint, providing the concluding paper to Part One and exploring much less-charted water.

Part Two of this text moves further into uncharted waters with an exploration of how the discussion on conscience is or is not taken up in other traditions. Jonathan Gorsky, George D. Chryssides and Ron Geaves undertake the tasks of examining Jewish, Islamic and Buddhist thinking in this area. It would seem very little had been written previously on the issue of conscience from the viewpoints of these traditions. These papers provide a scholarly and thought-provoking section not only for those within Judaism, Islam and Buddhism, but also for those within the Christian tradition who are open to the insights of others. The editor's greatest wish would be that this volume might initiate further debate in all traditions and lead the reader into a deeper appreciation of the breadth of human wisdom on this subject.

The editor would like to thank all the contributors for their support in this venture. She is particularly grateful to the last three contributors for their good-natured tolerance of her ignorance of the viewpoints from which they write. The editor also wishes to acknowledge the support of Robert Hannaford, the Series Editor, and that of John Hills for his endless patience and technical expertise in producing the manuscript. Finally, most sincere thanks must go to her husband, Bernard Hoose, for his never-failing loving support and encouragement.

Jayne Hoose
1998

Part One

1

A History of the Western Idea of Conscience

Helen Costigane SHCJ

Introduction

The idea of conscience in the western Christian tradition has
been one fraught with conflict over meaning and status. From
Paul's challenge to members of the Corinthian church over
their claims to have a clear conscience, to Luther's declaration at Worms that he could do nothing other than follow his
own conscience, to Kierkegaard's view that an authentic life
lies in taking responsibility for one's own conscience,
conscience and what we mean by it for the life of the individual has been the subject of much debate, and this discussion
continues to the present day. This chapter will consider a brief
history of the idea of conscience, exploring the Greek origins
of the word, its biblical usage, and issues arising from them.

Greek origins

The word 'conscience', derived from the Latin *conscientia*
(*con* meaning 'with', *scio* meaning 'I know'), is originally
found in a range of Greek texts from the sixth century BCE
to the seventh century AD as *syneidesis*. The main word in the
group – *synoida* – has a basic meaning of 'I know in common
with' (from *syn* and *eido*, 'with' and 'I know'). There are

other senses, among these being 'I bear witness'; 'I know well'; or 'I am conscious of'. *Syneidesis* itself generally refers to the goodness or badness of specific actions performed by an individual, but one who is in relationship with others. So, in the Greek fragments, these actions are seen mainly in terms of a breach of civic responsibility, such as receiving bribes, plundering public property, matricide, ignoble behaviour in war, and sexual corruption. The effect of *syneidesis*, or the awareness of a 'bad conscience' which knows that a bad action has been performed, is pain. However, this is no ordinary pain. Plutarch describes it in terms of being 'an ulcer in the flesh' which '... implants in the soul a remorse which never ceases to wound or goad it. Any other pain can be reasoned away, but this remorse is inflicted by reason',[1] and, therefore (he seems to be saying), not only is this pain more debilitating than any other that may be experienced, it is not possible to reason it away. Conscience therefore makes a judgement on actions performed, and inflicts pain when the individual becomes conscious of wrongdoing.

But what is the cause of this pain – in other words, where does conscience originate? In considering this question, it may be useful to take into account another of the extracts from the corpus of Greek writing within which *syneidesis* is found. In a fragment wrongly attributed to Epictetus, the origin of *syneidesis* is described in these terms:

> When we were children, our parents handed us over to a nursery-slave who should watch over us everywhere lest harm befall us. But when we are grown up, God hands us over to the *syneidesis* implanted in us, to protect us. Let us not in any way despise its protection, for should we do so, we shall be both ill-pleasing to God and have our own *syneidos* as an enemy.[2]

In this fragment, we see parallels drawn between the 'nursery slave' and *syneidesis*; it is something given, to the child by the parent, or to the adult by 'God' . This something is omnipresent and ever-vigilant, and its role can be described as being 'protection from harm', and therefore for the individual's own benefit. While the slave has parameters for action, his function being to guard and not to instruct, this seems to be paralleled in the very specific role attributed to *syneidesis*.

An important point is made with the idea that *syneidesis* only comes into operation with maturity. This suggests that the child has not yet developed the necessary capacities to make proper moral judgements. This is in line with Aristotle's views on the training needed to develop *nous* and *phronesis*. A brief review of his thought may be helpful here. Aristotle believed that *nous*, intelligence or intuitive reason, the starting point for the reasoning process, was the innate faculty which grasped the first principles for action and was a capacity which required training. This insight into principles Aristotle believed was made concrete by *phronesis* (practical wisdom), which helped the individual decide what ought to be done in a particular situation. However, not only were both important in making moral judgements, but the proper operation of *phronesis* depended on the individual possessing the necessary moral virtues – emotional dispositions arising from habit – enabling decisions to be made which were unclouded by emotion. Clearly, there is then a necessity for training and experience to facilitate development, and Aristotle's ideas on *nous* and *phronesis* seem to coincide with the idea that *syneidesis* comes into its own at an individual's maturity.

The nursery-slave need not be making a comment on the ethical content of the child's action, but this and the need for training need not suggest that *syneidesis* has no part to play in a child's development. However, following Aristotle's line of thought, it is more likely to be able to function in a mature adult, who has learned the appropriate virtues and who has been trained in the necessary capacities, than in a child in the early stages of development. For the mature adult, the external monitor has been internalized into *syneidesis*, so that individuals have the capacity to become conscious of wrongdoing themselves.

So we see in the Greek fragments the use of the word *syneidesis* which we in the Western Christian tradition understand as conscience. We see that it relates to the individual's knowledge of and judgement upon certain of his or her actions, that this awareness of wrongdoing inflicts a penalty which we might term guilt, and that this capacity for understanding is somehow implanted. This raises the question of how specifically this takes place, whether an individual is born with the capacity which is then developed, or whether he or she acquires it through lived experience, as it seems the child might do in relation to his or her experience of the nursery slave. Possible answers to this may be found in looking at the way in which conscience is alluded to, or directly spoken about, in the historical Christian texts. We continue by considering the biblical texts, before exploring how the ideas in these were developed by later Christian writers.

Biblical foundations

The Hebrew language has no specific word for conscience, though the idea of a judgement on actions performed is expressed by reference to the heart. The heart – meaning the inward part of a person as opposed to what is visible – is seen as the seat of the faculties and personality, and from it proceed thoughts and feelings, words, decisions, and actions. The Scriptures present the proper working of the heart in terms of seeking God, being in relationship with him, and listening to him. The idea of self-approval or self-reproach is seen in terms of the evaluation of actions within the context of this God-relationship. We saw that, in the Greek understanding, conscience seemed to be a function of reason, and that its pain was debilitating. The same idea is expressed in the Hebrew texts, where the effect of guilt on the individual is much more than feelings of reproach, remorse or contrition. Moreover, the workings of the heart, the seat of intelligence and decision making, can be affected. Wisd. 17. 11 expresses the idea of a guilty conscience which upsets the inner equilibrium, where the burdened conscience confuses reason and prevents it from discharging its proper function.

Similarly, nowhere in the Gospels is any specific term used for conscience, though the idea of heart is well represented. In Matthew's Gospel, there are 16 instances of the word. There are nine each in Mark and Luke, and five in John where the term is used in connection with the idea of inward disposition, orientation of life and awareness, the heart being the seat of intention which guides or inspires actions and thoughts. It is only when we get to the Epistles, notably the letters of

Paul, that we see the word for conscience, *syneidesis*, being used. Most of the 31 occurrences appear in the letters to the Corinthians. A brief review of these may be useful to show any development of ideas from the original Greek usage. The letters of Peter, and those to Timothy, display the idea of conscience in ways already seen in the Greek fragments. Here we see references to consciences that are 'good', 'clear' or 'pure'. The same ideas are seen in the Acts of the Apostles. The references in the Letter to the Hebrews do not suggest an extension of the original idea of conscience being something that inflicts pain because of actions done, but C. A. Pierce proposes that the writer of the letter is transposing it to a new setting. Placing it in the context of Jewish Christians falling away from faith in Christ and reverting to Judaism, the writer appears to be emphasizing that it is not a return to Judaic atonement ritual which will bring peace to a troubled conscience, but that it is only in the sacrificial death of Christ that a remedy may be found for the pain experienced.

It is Paul's letters to the church in Corinth which bring a greater awareness of how the Greek idea of *syneidesis* fits into the Christian context. In his discussion of meat sacrificed to idols, Paul points out that, for justification, it is not enough for an individual to say that his or her conscience is clear; the neighbour's conscience (especially if he or she is weak) must also be taken into consideration. In chapter 8 of the first letter, where there are four occurrences of *syneidesis* close together, Paul reminds the Corinthians that love, not knowledge (which they are clearly using to justify themselves) is what builds up the community. He notes their affirmation that there is only one God, but recognizes that there are still those who are struggling with the concept of monotheism and for whom false gods still remain part of their consciousness. This idea taints their perception of meat sacrificed to idols (the consumption of which is the issue in question), and so their conscience is vulnerable in a way in which the consciences of those who have grasped the idea of monotheism are not. In verses 10 and 12, Paul appears to challenge those who have the 'knowledge' (that there is one God, that a person cannot be defiled by food, and that the eating of idol meat is a neutral action) by inviting them to consider the effect of their actions on their neighbour's vulnerable conscience: 'Do you not think that his conscience, vulnerable as it is, may be encouraged to eat foods dedicated to false gods?'[3]

Conscience, in this context, seems to be more than awareness of wrongdoing, or something that pains because of this awareness. It becomes a judgement on actions performed, or about to be performed. But there is something more here. Those with vulnerable consciences perform an action, seeing that others do it, but are afflicted in a way in which the others are not. So there is a question of the knowledge or understanding which may be needed against which conscience may make correct judgements. Objectively, those who eat meat sacrificed to idols are doing nothing wrong, but the fact that Paul notes that some still suffer the pain of conscience on doing this suggests that there is some kind of problem requiring attention or education. Secondly, in addressing those who have robust consciences, Paul seems to be widening the scope of the moral content against which conscience makes its decisions; it is not enough to use moral codes and decide whether or not conscience is clear in reference to these. What is required now is a greater awareness of the neighbour in the context of love, a theme which Paul rehearses at other points in his writings.

Not only this, but within the Roman and Corinthian epistles, Paul is making what appears to be a key distinction between heart and conscience. In the letter to the Romans, Paul makes a reference to his conscience 'testifying' to himself that he is telling the truth as he sees it, his conscience being witness to his sincerity. At the same time, it is made clear in the text that he is not peaceful in heart, that he is experiencing some kind of emotional disturbance. The first point to be made, therefore, is that a clear conscience may not necessarily indicate a peaceful heart (though it is clear from other texts that both may be in a state of quietude at the same time). The division between the two is most clearly seen in his first letter to the Corinthians:

> It is true that my conscience does not reproach me, but that is not enough to justify me: it is the Lord who is my judge. For that reason, do not judge anything before the due time, until the Lord comes; he will bring to light everything that is hidden in darkness

and reveal the designs of all hearts. Then everyone will receive from God the appropriate commendation.[4]

Conscience itself, therefore, is not considered the sole tribunal of judgement; even though conscience may not be aroused, condemnation is still possible because of what lies within the heart, a point which echoes Paul's admonitions to the Corinthians.

So far, therefore, we have certain themes emerging from the consideration of the Greek and biblical texts: that there is a distinction between what we understand as heart and what we understand as conscience, though disequilibrium in one may affect the other; that conscience is somehow a function of reason, and that it is something which relates to the individual, but that its working cannot be seen in isolation and divorced from the wider community.

Heart, conscience and reason

The distinction between heart and conscience in the biblical texts is echoed by many of the early Christian writers. For Augustine, however, a disturbed conscience meant a disturbed heart, although there is a development in his thought in the relationship between the two. In Book One of the *Confessions* he writes: 'Certainly there is no knowledge more intrinsically true (*in cordibus suis*) than that which is written in our own consciences (*conscientia*), of not doing to others that which we would not suffer in ourselves'.[5] Augustine seems to be using *cor* (heart) to emphasise the fundamental nature of the knowledge found in the heart, an idea alluded to in Paul's reference in his letter to the Romans. This idea of 'knowledge written on the heart' is also expressed by Jerome, who speaks of the word of God being engraved on the heart. The question is how this word relates to the action of 'conscience' as we have already encountered it.

Earlier, we saw that conscience itself was a function of reason (in Greek terms) and a judgement made on a particular course of action, and that this understanding is not significantly altered in the biblical texts. Early Christian writers, most notably Augustine, did not make significant alterations to the understanding of this until Jerome, who was credited by the scholastics with having introduced a new word for the idea of a conscience which could never be lost: *synderesis*. This aspect of conscience which could never be erased was contrasted with *syneidesis*, that which could be lost through habitual disregard. The evidence as to whether Jerome intentionally drew the contrast between these two is inconclusive. At times he seems to be contradictory. What is significant is the emphasis that it is the action of God, through the Holy Spirit, which is necessary to keep the spark of conscience alive.

However, given that the scholastics believed there to be two aspects to conscience, it is worth considering how they saw both in terms of their relationship to each other. Thomas Aquinas used the idea of the practical syllogism to illustrate this. He argued that *synderesis* contained universal principles from which could be deduced, through the exercise of reason, those particular actions which were to be avoided or undertaken. So, for example, an illustration of this might be seen in terms of murder:

MAJOR PREMISE	SYNDERESIS	All evil must be avoided
MINOR PREMISE	REASON	Murder is evil
CONCLUSION	CONSCIENCE	Murder must be avoided

So, in Aquinas's terms, while *synderesis* is that which makes known to us general principles for action (which reflects the idea of the 'word written on the heart'), the other aspect of conscience is a function of practical reason which deals with specific issues. And we can see that, even if reason fails, the major premise remains unaltered. Jerome's account of the story of Moses killing an Egyptian is an example of this, where he sees that the operation of Moses' conscience had grown tarnished by his 'secular studies' and by the act of killing itself. However, the fact that reason and conscience both failed (or seemed to fail) did not eradicate his knowledge that there were certain principles for action in existence. His subsequent challenge by two Hebrews who seem to know of the killing is enough to reawaken that aspect of conscience which produces guilt. Therefore, although the question of whether *synderesis* is entirely synonymous with 'heart' may be open to debate, it is clear that God's word – in the form of general principles for action – is ineradicable in the human being, despite the distortions which may occur in reasoning.

In his writings Martin Luther added another aspect to Aquinas' syllogism with his definition of conscience (*Gewissen*) which he saw as working in conjunction with the mind in drawing conclusions about the performance of actions: 'As the mind judges, so the conscience dictates. The conscience always draws the conclusion, but the mind sets forth the minor premise... The major premise is always true, because it does not contradict the common sense of all men. If the minor premise is upheld, the conclusion follows'.[6]

We can consider the operation of conscience in Luther's terms in this way:

MAJOR PREMISE	COMMON SENSE	All sin is to be avoided
MINOR PREMISE	MIND	X is a sin
CONCLUSION	CONSCIENCE	To do/have done X is a sin.

Luther's problem with the church of his day was that what he thought were ridiculous observances, such as Friday abstinence or the requirement to wear certain liturgical vestments, had been elevated to such a level of impotence that conscience could do nothing other than conclude that non-observance was sinful. This bad teaching, he said, burdened people with traditions which were nothing to do with the faithful following of Christ, and caused misery for individual consciences (something which Luther himself had experienced as a young monk). His solution was the adherence of the individual conscience to the Word of God in the Scriptures which alone would produce certainty for conscience.

In the above, we see something of the relationship between heart, conscience, and reason, each distinct but interdependent (though in different ways, depending on perceptions). The ideas of John Henry Newman help us to begin to tie these together. Jerome was credited with coining a new word for conscience: the spark (which we might say lies within the heart) which can never be completely extinguished no matter how damaged the individual's ability to judge (or reason) has been affected by habitual sin. We also see Luther's very specific definition of conscience: something which, drawing on reason or common sense, judges the rightness or wrongness of a particular action. Newman's writings on conscience provide us with another and much wider idea of what conscience is for. While he acknowledges that conscience guides us and provides us with a sense of having done something wrong (with the realization of personal responsibility), for Newman it performs another – perhaps superior – function. Conscience speaks to us of the existence of God, and tells us something about what God is: 'in this special feeling, which follows on the commission of what we call right and wrong, lie the materials for the real apprehension of a Divine Sovereign and Judge'.[7]

Conscience tells us, then, that God exists, providing for the mind 'a real image of Him', and what God is in relation to ourselves – 'our Master ... our Creator and our Judge' whose presence is everywhere and who requires us to act in a certain way. Arising from this awareness, conscience then provides us with a rule of right and wrong 'as being His rule', and a code of moral duties. In his letter to the Duke of Norfolk, Newman writes:

> When Anglicans, Wesleyans, the various Presbyterian sects in Scotland, and other denominations among us, speak of conscience, they mean what we mean, the voice of God in the nature and heart of man, as distinct from the voice of Revelation. They speak of the principle planted within us, before we have had any training, although training and experience are necessary for its strength, growth and due formation. They consider it..to be the internal witness of both the existence and the law of God.[8]

Conscience is at the same time, in Newman's terms, both foundational (a sense of God implanted in the heart) and also a judgement, engaging reason, on actions undertaken in the light of this commitment to God.

Newman's ideas help us to draw together the three strands of heart, reason and conscience to identify two interrelated aspects of conscience. The first, which we might call 'Conscience 1 ' can be described as a 'foundational' conscience, the second 'Conscience 2' as a 'situational' conscience.

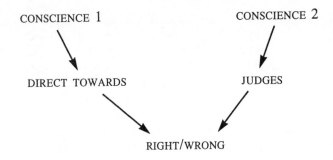

CONSCIENCE 1   CONSCIENCE 2

DIRECT TOWARDS   JUDGES

RIGHT/WRONG

The importance that both aspects remain in dialogue with each other is summed up by Kevin Kelly: 'My heart registers the basic direction in which I live my life, while, conversely, individual choices and decisions are the very life-blood of my heart and at times may even provide the occasion for a change of heart, as in key moments of conversion or personal corruption'.[9]

So we see that in the historical development of the idea of conscience, the original Greek idea of a pain inflicted by reason has been expanded to encapsulate not just this idea of judgement, but also the basic direction of an individual's life within which these judgements take place.

Conscience and the individual

Throughout the Christian tradition, there is an idea that conscience is very much something which relates to the individual. In the Greek sources, we see that the pain of conscience is something experienced by the individual who has transgressed, and no one else. This idea of the personality of conscience is most forcefully expressed by the life and writings of Martin Luther, whose declaration at the Diet of Worms (1521), which concluded his interrogation, is perhaps the best known example of a refusal to do something on grounds of conscience: 'I cannot and will not recant, for going against my conscience is neither safe nor salutary. I can do no other, here I stand. God help me.'[10]

Less dramatic (in terms of their consequences), but no less important, statements on this subject of the individuality of conscience have been made by such theologians as Søren Kierkegaard, John Henry Newman, and Karl Barth. Kierkegaard made his statements in the context of what he observed was happening in the church of his day, where he observed that people were avoiding responsibility for themselves by hiding in the crowd (the congregation) and refusing to stand up and be counted. He warned the church of his day that 'the fundamental corruption of our day consists in our having abolished personality...'[11] and he emphasized what he believed to be a fundamental fact of human existence, that one day the individual would be called upon, in eternity, to render an account of him or herself before God. Newman too emphasized this one-to-one relationship between God and the individual, and the very personal nature of conscience: 'Conscience is a personal guide, and I use it because I must use myself; I am as little able to think by any mind but my own as to breathe with another's lungs.'[12]

Barth, too, urged individual responsibility for, and obedience to, one's own conscience. Echoing Kierkegaard, he noted that individuals often chose to escape personal responsibility by pressuring the consciences of others to form a group, but he is clear that there is freedom to enter into a decision made by the collective conscience only if it truly concurs with our own: 'Even in relation to the neighbour, we are truly obedient only when his claim is also the claim of our own conscience'.[13]

So there has been a common strand in the history of conscience which stresses personal responsibility, a standing-apart from the collective stance if it conflicts with one's innermost truth, and, in the Christian tradition, the idea that one will have to render to God an account of the decisions made in conscience. Two very dramatic instances of this are seen in the lives of St Thomas More and Franz Jägerstätter. Emphasizing the central role that conscience plays in one's very humanity, More refused to swear an oath which would have conflicted with what he understood to be his innermost truth. This led to his execution for treason against King Henry VIII. Four hundred years later, Franz Jägerstätter was executed for his refusal of military service in Hitler's army. Thus the individuality of conscience – of one's personal responsibility before God – has been much more than just an idea for many individuals, but has had dramatic consequences for them and the communities within which they lived and died.

The role of the community in the formation of conscience

One of the problems we are faced with, if we understand our narrower definition of conscience as an exercise of the faculty of reason, is that we know it can fail from time to time (as we saw in the case of Moses). To rely solely on conscience, then, without reference to any external authority, is equally as problematic as over-dependence on that authority. In his letters to the Corinthians, Paul urged the members of the church to have consideration for those who were weak, stressing that the exercise of personal conscience should not take place without some regard for the effect it had on other people. So there is already present within the early Christian community the idea that conscience is somehow shaped by reference to others.

Augustine of Hippo develops the idea of the necessity of some kind of outside reference because of what might be termed an epistemological handicap: the effect of original sin on the ability of the individual to know what might be the right thing to do. This tendency to sin and ignorance (because of the individual's fallen nature) needed some kind of restraint placed on it, and Augustine saw the remedy for this in belonging to the Church, within which is found the Holy Spirit. The need to belong to a faith community is stressed by other writers too, though each has different emphases. For all his stress on the individual, Kierkegaard recognised that the Church had a role in rescuing individuals from isolated subjectivity, where the possibility existed that inwardness (the individual in an inwardly reflective stance) might end up embracing what he called a 'finite fixed idea' rather than the truth. Giving positive assent to the Church's doctrine and organization, he fixed the boundaries of relationship in these terms: 'In the highest religious form, the individual relates himself first to God and then to the congregation: but this first relationship is the highest, though the individual does not neglect the latter'.[14]

Newman spoke of a balanced relationship between the Church's teaching, ruling and ministering offices, which would avoid arbitrary commands, unbridled and untheological enthusiasm, and unfettered (and unhelpful) theological speculation. A balanced interdependence between these three functions would ensure that the exercise of pastoral judgement by the ordained ministry and the religious experience of ordinary Christians would be in creative tension with each other. It would also avert demands for an absolute obedience to authority, to which Newman was opposed because of his convictions concerning the integrity of conscience.

The content of teaching

Throughout the history of western Christianity, however, there have been different emphases on the sources of wisdom against which conscience must make its judgements. At different points in time the importance of the natural law and reason, tradition and leadership, and the Bible have been differently stressed. Aquinas believed natural law to be a participation in the eternal law of God, and that through reflecting on one's natural inclinations, reason would disclose certain general precepts: that there are inbuilt dispositions to preserve life, procreate, educate children, live in society, and seek truth. However, he reflects Augustine's idea of an epistemological handicap when he speaks of the ability (or inability) fully to understand the law: 'as time went on, sin too began to take more hold on man, to such an extent that, with his reason darkened by sin, the precepts of the law of nature were not enough for living rightly, and they had to be determined in the written law'.[15]

This darkening of the capacity for human knowledge was remedied through the teaching of the Scriptures, a point which is put rather more forcefully by Luther, who saw that following a religion of conscience could terrify the individual, because we can never achieve knowledge of God, or what he may be asking of us, by our own efforts. True teaching is what is needed, and this can only be found in the Word of God: 'God wants our conscience to be certain and sure that it is pleasing to Him. This cannot be done if the conscience is led by its own feelings, but only if it relies on the Word of God'.[16] Only in the Scriptures will we find what God is truly like, a merciful judge to those who acknowledge themselves as sinners; knowledge of the Word must therefore be the believer's chief concern.

Karl Barth, too, recognised the dependence of conscience on the Scriptures, as he believed that it was only through the Word of God that humankind could know what was good:

> A conscience which tells us the truth has to be the conscience which is captive to the Word of God, and this captivity has to signify no more and no less than its elevation to participation in the truth itself. Our self-accusing and self-excusing thoughts cannot remain on their own. This self-dialogue has to have a share in the dignity and truth of the Word of God.[17]

However, even with this emphasis on the Bible, there is no sense among these writers that interpretation is purely subjective. There is general agreement that good teaching is needed at the same time. An example can be seen in Paul's letter to the Corinthians, which casts him in a teaching role, the picture created being one of the exercise of charism rather than an authoritarian office. Augustine too recognised the need for a teaching function, seeing that God's Spirit is at work within the Church. Kierkegaard, though scathing about the example given by the clergy of his day and their witness to the gospel, recognised the importance of a guiding and teaching function in rescuing individuals from an isolated subjectivity. This too was emphasized by Newman who saw the Church as guarding and preserving a substantive message from God. Luther, however, pointed out most forcefully the dangers of a sinful church which loses its way, where the teaching becomes distorted and causes misery and despair among ordinary consciences.

But what is the content of this teaching? Tradition represents the accumulated wisdom of the community in living the gospel, and along with official church teaching, incorporates the thought of major theologians, saints, and prophetic voices.

This community wisdom has been subject to constant development as new challenges have been faced within the Christian community, and examples of this can be seen in the evolution of Just War Theory, Augustine's attempt to respond to the necessity of protecting society against an unjust aggressor, and its subsequent refinements in the context of the nuclear age; the shift in stance from a one-time acceptance of slavery to its condemnation; the discussion about sustaining life in the event of brain-death; and the whole area of gender-related issues, with the emphasis of the present day on the need for the community to listen to, and incorporate, the experience of women in formulating ethical demands.

So we can see that conscience has various sources of wisdom against which it makes its judgement on the rightness or wrongness of actions performed. Immediate instruction is given through reason in terms of general principles for action, but the noetic problem brought about by the Fall impairs the ability of reason to see the whole picture. The revelation of the Bible (God's word) and its subsequent interpretation through the teaching faculty within the Church makes good this defect, but it is clear that for some writers the first is of more importance than the second. So we see that in terms of the situational conscience identified earlier, additional teaching is needed to overcome the impairment caused by original sin.

Summary

In this chapter, we have considered how the word which we understand as conscience originated, how the idea has evolved, and how conscience relates to the individual and to the community. It is clear that many writers today see it as a much wider idea than a pain arising from an awareness of wrongdoing; one example of this being Lewis K Rambo, who writes that conscience is:

> The complex human capacity, utilising people's understanding of moral life and their decision making ability, to live in conformity with those principles it deems acceptable and good. In a morally informed and psychologically balanced person, the conscience

serves as a guide or a monitor of life, enabling the individual to evaluate and choose potential courses of action and thought in the light of his or her values and commitments.[18]

This definition sums up the ideas expressed by various writers on conscience; that there is a foundational aspect in terms of awareness of general principles; that it relates to the individual within the context of a community which has articulated something of those principles; and that it is a judgement on individual actions in the light of the commitment given to those values.

Notes

1   Plutarch, quoted by C. A. Pierce, 'Conscience in the New Testament', *Studies in Biblical Theology, Number 15* (SCM Press, London, 1955), extract 49, p. 47.
2   Pierce, *Ibid*, p. 51: a fragment wrongly attributed to Epictetus by Meibomius.
3   1 Cor. 8.10 (New Jerusalem Bible).
4   1 Cor. 4.4–5 (New Jerusalem Bible).
5   Augustine quoted from H. Chadwick (tr.), *Saint Augustine's Confessions* (Oxford University Press, 1991), Confessions Book 1, 18.29.
6   Luther, D. Martin Luthers Werks: Kritische Gesamtausgabe (WA) 25.39.16, 25–26, quoted by Zachman, *The Assurance of Faith: Conscience in the Theology of Martin Luther and John Calvin* (Fortress Press, Minneapolis, 1993), p. 24.
7   John Henry Newman, *An Essay in Aid of a Grammar of Assent* (Longmans, Green & Company, London, 1939), p. 105.
8   Letter to the Duke of Norfolk, quoted by I. Ker, *The Genius of Henry Newman* (Clarendon Press, Oxford, 1989), p. 263.
9   Kevin T. Kelly, *New Directions in Moral Theology: The Challenge of Being Human* (Geoffrey Chapman, London, 1992), p. 17.
10 Heiko A. Oberman, *Luther: Man between God and the Devil* (Fontana Press, 1993), p. 203.
11 Howard V. and Edna H. Hong, *Søren Kierkegaard's Journals and Papers, 6 Volumes,* (Bloomington, 1967), journal 3229.
12 *Grammar of Assent*, pp. 389–390.
13 Karl Barth, *Ethics (tr. by Geoffrey W. Bromiley),* (T & T Clark, Edinburgh, 1981), p. 484.

14 Kierkegaard, journal 4110.
15 The Dominican Fathers, *The Summa Theologica of St Thomas Aquinas, The English Translation,* (Burns, Oates & Washbourne, London, 1921), Summa Theologiae 3a, q. 61, art. 3, ad 2.
16 Luther WA 14 644. 22–24, quoted by Zachman, *op cit*, p. 28.
17 Barth, *op. cit.*, p. 477.
18 Lewis K. Rambo, 'Conscience' in Alan Richardson and John Bowden (eds), *New Dictionary of Christian Theology* (SCM Press, London, 1983), p. 119.

2

Against Conscience: a Protestant View

Dave Leal

Introduction

How necessary is conscience to the living of a good life? The contention advanced in this paper is that conscience, or at least *consciousness* of conscience, has been given a far more elevated rôle in Christian moral thinking than it actually deserves. It has become, at times, a threat to the claim that our justification before God is ultimately a justification based upon faith in Christ, rather than upon our own sincere adherence to our conscientiously held beliefs. The concentration on particular questions (such as, 'are we right to act in accordance with conscience, even when mistaken?') has given centre stage to a view of moral existence in which it is the goal of moral thinking to arrive at moral judgements; the judgements are then open to acceptance or rejection by 'the will', perceived as a kind of 'faculty' or 'power' of the mind; and we are morally justified only in so far as we 'will' in accordance with the dictates of conscience. 'Justification' appears then, whether in an alternative or an auxiliary sense, to be based on 'right willing', on falling in with the dictates of conscience.

Now, there is certainly *something* in this which deserves to be taken seriously. After all, the most intellectually demanding moral questions are ones where we really *do* seem to need to think things through and come to a judgement, aware that we may be mistaken. In terms of moral psychology, the awareness of the capacity for (and, potentially, the seriousness of) any error gives us a certain detachment from the conclusion of our process of judgement. We are not *sure* that this is the right thing to do; to do it requires a choice, which may sometimes be called 'an act of will'. The process of moral reasoning which arrives at the (fallible) judgement about 'what ought to be done' is (at least a part of) what many Christian authors have thought of as conscience. Much of the goal of moral education may well be to educate conscience in this sense, that is, educating to think through questions of good and evil, right and wrong, in particular and unclear cases.

I do not want to dispute any of this, but I do want to question the tendency of authors to make this a kind of paradigm for moral life. It is sometimes made to appear that *all* our morally responsible actions should be the result of judgements of will on an abstract proposition about how one ought to behave, a proposition presented to the will by 'conscience'. Thus, in such accounts, the 'will' comes to have a central position in morality; it plays a pivotal role in the conversion of moral thought into moral action. It is certainly true that a 'flawed will' has been one common explanation for human moral incapacity. One *might* read Paul's comments in Rom. 7.7f as the claim that correct moral *knowledge* can be accompanied by feebleness or incapacity of *willing*. The obvious and urgent question of how moral integrity may be brought about appears to look like a question about the health of a part of the mind called the 'will'.

Protestant thinkers have been divided concerning the ultimate theological significance and status of the will. The controversy concerning whether conversion to Christian faith is best seen as a choice of truth by the converted person (an act of will), or as the submission of a creature to a call from its Creator in a way which (whatever its conscious biographical components) is quite other than a choice, or at least a choice *by the creature itself,* has been seen often enough as the question whether an act of will is a 'work'. If we answer that it *is,* this appears to threaten the central insight that salvation is not by works.

What, then, about good works done after salvation? Are these matters of which we may be proud, and take the credit? There is, after all, no small amount of 'reward-language' in the New Testament where good works are concerned. If we take the vocation to good works seriously, it can then sometimes appear that we are 'saved' by a particular and mysterious act of God's choice, but subsequently precipitated in a slightly disconnected way into a radically self-absorbed duty to live a moral life, which is to say, a life lived in accordance with the dictates of conscience. It is as if salvation is claimed to have healed the will, and made it possible to choose the good and avoid the bad.

Yet it is by no means obvious that this model of reason-and-will is a workable one. We may be worried, too, by the disconnection of salvation from growth in moral life, which is surely one aspect of sanctification. Good living could be said, after all, to be not so much founded on a particularly developed capacity for the *willing* or *choosing* of abstract 'moral facts', as on the development of a more organic *capacity to do* the right and good, and to avoid the evil. In short, what is missing when will plays a central part in the picture of moral life is a concern with moral *character*. Yet the more we play up the theme of moral character, the less self-consciousness appears to attach to our 'moral experience'. When it was suggested above that conscience-and-will may play a part in *some* of our moral life, it was admitted that these will be moments of moral unclarity or uncertainty. Where the good is obvious, the good person does it, not conscious of 'thinking it through', not conscious of any 'act of will' at all. Where there is the possibility of evil action, the good person is not the one who, noticing the possibility, rejects it by an act of will; he or she is likely not to notice it at all.[1]

This is not to say that we can necessarily dispense with the concepts of conscience and of will in giving an account of the moral life, even where all is 'working well' and there are no doubts or uncertainties. They will not, though, under such circumstances, be matters of the *conscious* life of the individual moral agent, and one part of the aim of this investigation is to show something of the way in which this may be so. Much of the time, the good moral agent may not be conscious of 'willing' at all. If we were to ask the theological question whether the 'cause' of a person's good actions lies in the individual or in God – as certain sensibilities common enough in Protestant Christianity may well ask – then the response ought, by rights, to be a certain bemusement. Where, after all, did the creature and its sanctification come from? Good human living is living which gives glory to its creator by demonstrating an absolute transparency of its own actions to the desire and purpose of God, so we may properly speak of a causal *transparency* of the holy life to the will of the divine. Yet it is the creature *itself* which is sanctified; good living is not an *overriding* of its will, and it is not a puppet. The goal of sanctification is in part that we might be, quite unselfconsciously, what we are made to be in the arena of moral living; that we should be, without consciousness of, or pride in, our own achievements, the immediate cause of our own right living.[2]

The sources of 'conscience', and some metaethical reflections

As is well enough known, the word 'conscience' comes from a compound of two Latin terms, *cum* and *scio*. *Scio* and related words form the historical root for English words such as 'science'. *Scio* concerns knowledge, and means 'I know'. With the addition of *cum* (in the compound it becomes *con-*), *conscio* amounts to 'I know with'. There is a parallel in Greek, where *sun* is 'together with' and *oida* is the verb (from this group we get words like 'idea' and related terms). So alongside *conscio* we have the Greek word *sunoida,* both apparently carrying the sense of 'I know (together) with'. However, there are relatively early examples of uses of these terms which appear to have lost something of the element of 'together' or 'along with'. C. S. Lewis gives examples from Diogenes Laertius (late second or first half of third century AD), Plutarch (*c.*46–*c.*120), and the Septuagint, examples where the meaning appears to be something like 'awareness', 'knowledge *of*' (rather than 'with'), or even simply 'thought'.[3] Timothy Potts remarks that it is a very recent development which clearly distinguishes between conscience and consciousness[4] but even if this is right it can only be a matter of degree. There is no reason in principle to believe that users of the relevant vocabulary would be unable to account for the distinct kinds of application to which they were put. Professor Lewis speaks of two 'branches' developing from the Greek and Latin roots. One is what we might think of as the expected form of development, and he terms it the 'together' branch. In the other, the 'together' or 'along with' sense is diminished or quite lost. This he dubs the 'weakened' branch.

Intriguingly, the 'together-sense' appears at first sight pretty remote from many obvious uses of both 'conscience' and 'conscious' as they are used in modern English. The 'weakened' branch diverges on the former side (conscience) to a kind of basic moral awareness, and on the latter (conscious) to a more general sense of 'awareness'. It might be noted that the uses of 'conscious' cover a spectrum of senses, from 'sentience' through reflexive self-awareness, including 'thinking' along the way. Cats and dogs can be said in some sense to be 'conscious'. Equally, though, the word might be used to *distinguish* human mental experience from that of other animals. The examples of the together-sense which Lewis cites are often ones which may be misread by a modern speaker of English, who is not alive to the dynamics – the vestige of the 'together-sense' – of the meaning of the word in this context. He offers the following from Jane Austen's *Northanger Abbey* (chapter 30): Henry Tilney is introduced to Mrs Morland 'by her conscious daughter'. This is not telling the reader that the daughter is currently self-aware or self-conscious (as opposed, say, to having fainted or been struck on the head with a large mallet and thus rendered *un*conscious). No, 'She was *conscious* in exactly the classical sense; knowing much which her mother did not know about Henry and her own relations to him, she was in a secret, shared a knowledge with him. This is '*being conscious*'; but you can also '*look conscious*', look like a conspirator or accomplice'.[5]

The primary historical sense of 'conscious' lies in the private sharing of some piece of knowledge. Obviously, as secrets and confidences may tend to be matters of shame more often than benevolence or approbation (even though the latter may be common enough) 'conscious' in this sense may carry an expected negative overtone, though *particular* uses need not be negative. It is through the capacity of the individual to 'know one's own deeds and thoughts', to be privy to one's *own* secrets, that the self may become, reflexively, the paradigm case of (non-metaphorical) 'con-sciring'. There is, though, only a moral tone to this *at all* in the sense that secrets shared with others are likely to be of dark or suspicious matters. Given that my self-consciousness is an apparently natural part of what it is to be human, this particular use of 'conscious' might even in general be said to have no more moral force than the use of 'conscious' in any current sense would imply.

A change comes, however, with the involvement of a further element of moral psychology. It may be that our self-*awareness* of our actions is in itself a neutral matter. The actions *themselves* may be very far from neutral, however, and the capacity to see the self as an object of awareness leads on to the self passing judgement upon itself. Strictly speaking, as Lewis notes, this is a distinct operation: the metaphor of the lawcourt, so readily employed as an image of moral judgement, places the individual as judge, and also as witness, two quite distinct relations and yet both borne in relation to the same self. The *witness* functions in the classical tradition of 'consciring', bearing witness to 'the facts'. The *judge,* aware of the moral status of what is presented, pronounces a verdict. Lewis suggests that the language of conscience becomes confused; these two quite distinct features each become associated with the same group of words. An individual may now speak of 'having a bad conscience', when existing under a state of self-judgement. Lewis takes the tendency of the medieval theologians to work with two vocabularies here as significant for this distinction; he holds that they tend to use '*synderesis*' (a Latinising of the Greek word) when thinking of awareness of moral principles, and '*conscientia*' tends to be used for awareness that one has done such-and-such.

In fact, though, the historical situation is more complex.[6] Thomas Aquinas, in whom the distinction is most famously drawn, may well claim (as Lewis remarks) that he is conforming to 'the common use of language',[7] but this might be misleading; one wonders if Thomas is thinking in part of something like 'the common use *interpreted by theological precedent'*, though he is also keen to stress an etymological justification. The theological precedent has a significant background, clearly sketched by Timothy Potts,[8] in the attempt to resolve an apparent inconsistency in Jerome's commentary on the book of Ezekiel. The 'resolution' of this inconsistency was based around the positing of a (historically unsound) distinction between *synderesis* and *conscientia,* the former coming to constitute some form of primary awareness of moral principles, the latter relating to application in particular cases. The importance of the history of this development is, as Dr Potts suggests, quite independent of its accuracy in interpreting Jerome; it opens up a variety of explorations of the moral psychology of the individual which may be fruitful even if they were initially based upon a mistake (either by Jerome or someone who copied his manuscript). The authors themselves tend, whilst giving different accounts for the belief, to hold that one's *synderesis* – knowledge of basic principles – is necessarily correct. Errors can occur in application (though Thomas appears to hold that the more direct the application, the less opportunity there is for error); *conscientia* can err, but *synderesis* cannot.[9]

What can we learn from this account? We may see that to be 'conscious' in the weakened sense of pure 'awareness' or the slightly richer sense of 'self-awareness' is a necessary *precursor* to the exercise of *conscientia* in the technical sense of moral thinking. We may also note that the 'sharing' expressed in the classical sense of *conscio* might be extended, by a suitable understanding of the origin of moral value, to include *synderesis* also. If the 'knowledge' implicit in *synderesis* is justified as knowledge by its conformity to God's determination of moral value, then we may be said to 'know along with' him.

Germain Grisez helpfully distinguishes three approaches to the nature of conscience which might be thought to map on to this account by altering the perception of this element of '*synderesis*'.[10] In effect, the three rival accounts posit distinct origins for the 'precepts' inherent in *synderesis,* which we might call 'personal', 'cultural' and 'absolute'. In the first, the origin and justification of the principles lies in the need to conform and gain affection. This is the realm of the superego, the internalizing of the commands of parents and other author-ity figures. In the second, the perception of norms is governed by social convention and prejudice. It is worth noting that neither the radically subjective superego nor the relativistic reliance upon human culture and community to provide norms are *guaranteed* inevitably to diverge in their *particular* content from the third possibility, that of a genuinely 'objective' arena of moral value. It may be that the child is dominated by the internalized demands of parents; it may be that no mature adult is completely free from the arbitrary elements in his cultural context which are presented as if they are 'objective moral norms'. The task of growing in moral maturity is the connecting of moral perception with true moral norms, trans-forming partial and relative conscience into right-functioning conscience, conscience which judges according to moral truth.

This account is certainly helpful. It results, in Professor Grisez's work, in the claim that 'The Church is interested in conscience only in the third sense, as the ability to know moral truth'.[11] It follows that 'Given this understanding of conscience, it is true by definition that one ought to follow one's conscience'. Necessarily so, for this is simply saying that one ought to do what one ought to do! Central questions remain, of course. Even in the absence of scepticism about the *existence* of moral truth, there might be concern about whether that truth is *obtainable* (that is, knowable), especially so the more impressed we are by the divergence of deeply held moral convictions.[12]

A further issue needs to be raised. What would it be like to have a completely right-functioning conscience? Presumably, one could act without wondering or fearing whether what one did would be right; right living would not be a feature of potentially fallible calculation any more than of pure accident. Professor Grisez's account implies at least this much. Right conscience constitutes both an awareness of moral truth and some kind of awareness *that it is* moral truth, though the nature of this 'awareness' is actually at the centre of any thor-ough investigation of conscience. If this is right, it raises serious questions about the goal of moral life as regards self-consciousness. We might usefully seek a comparison with other areas of life where criteria for 'success' are available and can be spelt out. The athletics coach may be able to improve the technique of the high jumper by suggesting how the foot should be placed on take-off. The athlete spends hours in self-absorbed and radically self-conscious attempts to 'get it right'. Yet ironically once it *is* right, the fullest criterion for the appropriation of the new aspect of technique is that it becomes absolutely unthinking. Indeed, subtleties may intrude which improve the execution, which the coach has never imagined, and of which the athlete is unaware at a conscious level and is incapable of expressing precisely in anything other than performance; thus the dialectic of theory and practice works itself out. And all this time the coach is unable to jump so much as half the height of his pupil; knowing much in theory, his body permits little in practice.

How far can we accept this as a satisfactory parallel? We may immediately be concerned at any suggestion that someone could be 'coached in morality' by a person who was unable to live a moral life. Perhaps some undergraduates have wondered whether teachers of 'practical ethics' may not sometimes be moral rogues! Yet it seems scarcely intelligible that someone could know the good and yet not do it. Or at least so it has seemed to those who have regarded the content of consistent *moral* action as action in accord with *interest*.[13] Now, of course, one might make one of at least two responses here.

The first is to suggest that there are indeed a variety of forms in which 'moral incapacity' may be exhibited, *even in the possession of moral knowledge*. These will at least include all of the standard issues in discussions of '*akrasia*', somewhat unhappily 'translated' in many accounts as 'weakness of will'. A second and distinct move would be to deny *any* direct link with 'interest' at all, and to attempt to render morality a matter of pure 'duty'. Again, this possibility coincides with a familiar axis of philosophical discussion, this time the distinction of 'categorical' and 'hypothetical' imperatives, giving them the 'Kantian' labels. 'Hypothetical' imperatives are those obligations which only become relevant for us in the light of some project which we (hypothetically) happen to have; 'you ought to catch the early train (if you want to be home in time to watch the football)'. 'Categorical' ones depend on no such further

description of a 'project'; they are, in this sense, *pure* imperatives. If there is a sterility in *this* debate, it probably comes
from the misperception of what is a perfectly proper distinction
in moral thinking, what we might term the distinction between
restricted and universal motivation. This comes out in the way
in which purified 'duty' and 'obligation' become radically
detached from concerns with and investigation of 'interest'.

It is quite possible to construe interest so narrowly, and
against such a limited horizon, that determining 'the right
thing to do' becomes feasible by virtue of a kind of moral
calculus. The *content* of moral motivation is reduced to the
simple 'because it's the right thing to do', and there is a
severe reduction of what may be termed 'moral expectation';
anything might, in appropriate circumstances, be right and so
be something we are called on to do. This is obviously true in
utilitarianism, where the right action is determined solely by
the capacity to promote pleasure and minimize pain, and in its
putative Christian counterpart in a situational ethic such as that
of Joseph Fletcher.[14] Intriguingly, these two polarities,
Kantianism and utilitarianism, both point towards a particularly cerebral vision of good human existence in the moral
sphere, an arena in which 'conscience' as a kind of inner taunt
against superficially desired action can be given a good deal
of elbow-room.

It is not enough to say that 'the demands of morality' simply
are categorical, as if no reason beyond a certain kind of
logical purity could be given for them. We *may* say: given the
kind of creation made by God, it is a matter of hypothetical
necessity that he should require or forbid such-and-such of his
creatures. There *may* be no *logical* reason why the finest detail
of that creation and the consequently inevitable demands and
limits for human action could not be known to us, but the relation of creature to creator is such that *his* special creative
knowledge and perception of 'interest' is definitive, and
human perception always a matter of discernment of this
'given'. In this sense, the truths of morality meet *us* as categorical, as truths relative to no other criterion than the
consistent and holy will of God. And in this sense, of course,
we never 'know' in moral thinking in the same way as that in
which we are 'known'. This obviously holds great significance

for any understanding which we might hope to reach of the nature of conscience as 'knowing-with'.

One final and important remark in this excursion into metaethics: there is an obvious and profound asymmetry between that which is 'wrong' and that which is 'not-wrong'. In utilitarian thinking, this tends to appear as the judgement that some one action is contextually right because it has maximal utility (or, rarely, some range of actions are equally right alternatives, sharing equal utility). It is more common in Christian moral thinking to see wrong actions identified and prohibited, whilst an arena of 'all-right' actions is left open to the individual. This asymmetry will figure in our developing discussion of the 'judgements of conscience' below.

Classifications of conscience

It would be wrong, of course, to imagine that the word 'conscience' is used in just one way. A number of suggestions of different uses have been contained in the account above. It appears that there are at least four uses which might be isolated and identified:

(a)   The (purely) *reactive* conscience. This is exhibited in some New Testament examples, and constitutes one standard usage of the term. It refers to the use of the word to characterize the response of the self to an action or decision already past. Having done something, the agent reflects (perhaps spontaneously and involuntarily) on the action, producing a particular affective response (perhaps guilt, shame, or remorse). It may be that the 'reaction' has something of the character of what we might term 'moral judgement', though the appropriateness of that expression might be questioned. What concerns us more *for the moment* is whether our list of characteristic affective responses ought to confine itself to the negative ones.

   The issue here might be partially related to Lewis's remarks, noted above, about the negative presumptions of 'consciring'. Lewis, we recall, regards a central part of the history of the word-group to which 'conscience' belongs as the sharing of secrets; and whilst not *all* secrets are matters of guilt or shame, most probably are. Is the reactive sense of conscience especially concerned with *negative* response to actions? We might approach this question by asking whether an action followed by (say) an involuntary glow of pride or approval would *count* as an example of 'reactive conscience'. I suspect that it would not, and that reactive conscience is purely a phenomenon of negative affective response. It can, however, be seen as existing in a kind of continuity with certain other senses of the word.

(b)   The *minimal* conscience. It seems clear that no sustained experience of affective reaction to *past* actions or decisions (even if just negative ones) could be borne without this contributing to a formation of character with respect to *future* acts. Even purely at the level of conditioning, the painful memory of past guilt is likely to prevent one from being ready to perform an action of a similar type again. Of course, there are issues here about what is to count as an action 'of a similar type'. I have 'learnt' by the negative reactions I experience that I should not cause pain, an education which might easily prevent me from doing so in future even in cases where immediate pain may prevent harm or promote future benefits. Imagining our attention restricted to the purely affective reaction, it appears that our responses to certain actions might well create a kind of background against which future decisions to act are made. This account, like that of reactive conscience upon which it is parasitic, is at least ostensibly 'sub-rational'. Where we need to take *reason* into account very seriously in characterizing it is in identifying what is to count as the right *kind* of affective response, and the relevant *order* of act. Here we reach one of the limits which cannot be investigated further in this essay; it is highly relevant that, as Simon Blackburn says, 'It is notable that each emotion [he refers specifically to guilt and shame] is only easily characterized in moral terms'.[15] This is obviously not the same as saying that one can only experience these emotions once one has a worked-out moral theory: but if Professor Blackburn is correct, it does imply that to give a proper *account* of guilt and shame will be part of the much larger task of giving an account of morality *as such*.

(c)   The *articulate* conscience. Beyond the characterization of conscience as purely reactive, or as an affective element in character formation, we have the sense of conscience as (according to Thomas Aquinas) 'the mind of a man making moral judgements'. Here, 'the mind' is understood at least as the process of conscious reasoning towards or about action. The narrowest conception or image of this is probably that of the lawcourt, an image which occurs in the New Testament, and which has been mentioned above. This is frequently discussed in the literature, though not always with the attention to the question of available verdicts which might be passed. Typically, the focus is on the question of the 'judgement to be passed on the self', whether guilty or not guilty; a typical English translation[16] of Rom. 2.15 includes 'accusing or else defending them', though the form of this 'defending' is a little unclear. Typically a lawcourt may be required to judge whether an individual did an action; the image of conscience-as-lawcourt is more like the case where a court, having decided that such-and-such was indeed done by the accused, has to decide on its status (whether the killing was murder or manslaughter, whether the words written were libellous or not). So we may ask: admitting that I was angry, should I regard the anger as wrong?

It is generally the business of an English court to decide a defendant guilty or not guilty (with the grounds for verdicts of 'not guilty' being wider than simply that something was not actually done, or that it turned out to be legally permitted – cases of diminished responsibility may figure here). Scots law has available to it in certain contexts the further verdict of 'not proven', and it may actually be that the lawcourt metaphor of conscience could be usefully extended at least so far as that. Frequently our own guilt or innocence, beyond the bare availability of the facts of the case, the 'what was done', is a matter over which we are not competent to judge one way or the other. Still, the verdicts remain couched in terms which relate to the priority of concern with guilt. Perhaps we can imagine individuals *praising* themselves or *congratulating* themselves for some action; but this is some distance from the expected content of the lawcourt metaphor.

The richest conception of articulate conscience has already been sketched in the account of the medieval development above. Here, with the discrimination of fundamental principles and application to specific cases, conscience achieves a measured distance from the purely reactive sense, and becomes the arena within which decisions regarding future actions may be reached. Thomas's 'mind of a man making moral judgements' might, then, be heard in a correspondingly richer sense, as including the judgement that an action may be positive, required, obligatory, or permissible, legitimate, neutral, as well as wrong, ruled out, prohibited. We shall examine this sense of 'articulate conscience' further below.[17]

(d)   Conscience as *reflexive moral character*. This is a minor sense, and parasitic upon the above forms, especially perhaps 'minimal conscience'. It is beautifully illustrated in a few lines from Arthur Miller's autobiography, as follows (the speakers are Hedda Rosten and Arthur Miller, and the two people spoken of are Miller and his wife Marilyn Monroe):

Rosten: "You are both very guilty", she said one after-noon as we had our teas together in the music room.
Miller: "I can't understand why."
Rosten: "You both have the same conscience."
Miller: "What does that mean, exactly?"
Rosten: "You can't accept what you don't think you deserve; you take exception to each other when it was supposed to be perfect. So you're punishing yourselves."[18]

Here 'having the same conscience' appears to mean some-thing like 'having the same attitude and relationship to oneself'. This use appears to be parasitic on a long process of development in the use of the word. It reduces the 'process' of conscience to an instant, a synchronic snapshot of response-to-self viewed as an aspect of character.

This classification makes no pretences to being complete or definitive. It specifically ignores, what surely deserves to be ignored in classification, the 'voice of God' view of conscience. It does so because such a conception of conscience imposes upon the individual who experiences the apparently divine claim a burden of discrimination and discernment (is this *really* God speaking?) which simply relocates the problems of reception of knowledge and truth. We shall return to this issue at a later stage of our inquiry. The classification offered is presented in part to make us aware of the range of uses which the word 'conscience' is subject to, and also to alert us to the problems of producing any simple answer to the question of whether Jesus had a conscience. With this much background, we move to a more direct confrontation with that question.

Did Jesus have a conscience?

Let us begin by dismissing a very familiar use for the denial that someone has a conscience. This is a kind of 'third-party' use, and is parasitic upon the second of Professor Grisez's distinctions of conscience, the cultural-norms view. Imagine, for example, a notorious adulterer. Someone wishing to pass judgement on the person might declare 'he has no conscience'. This declaration actually appears to mean something like 'he does not conform to the right standards'. We need not probe how much or what kind of content the word 'right' needs to have. The crucial matter is the judgement of lack of conscience by virtue of criteria of external conformity. The person who made the judgement 'he has no conscience' *might* be willing to retract the judgement if convinced that the person involved felt great guilt at his infidelity ('but even so I just cannot prevent myself'), but it does not seem that this evidence of the presence of 'reactive' conscience, as we have termed it, necessarily counts against the denial of conscience in the relevant sense.[19] Here, then, is a potential ground for denial that Jesus had a conscience. He is overheard pronouncing woes on the religious leaders and elders, or 'answering his mother back' at a wedding, or seen overturning the tables in the temple and causing a commotion. Tutting voices are heard, murmuring 'he has no conscience'.

This is *not,* though, especially relevant to our purposes. As set up, the example concerns the degree of conformity of behaviour to social norms of a relevant kind. Whilst we might indeed imagine raising the question of conformity of character and behaviour to a morally objective criterion, it is hardly possible to do so in the case of Jesus, if we accept the tradition of Jesus-as-sinless (see particularly Heb. 5.8–9). There will, of course, need to be some clarification on these points below. For the present, we simply note that this particular form of *third-party* evaluation is not relevant for our purposes, because it relies upon a morally *relativistic* conception of conscience. We might more usefully examine the question whether Jesus had a conscience in relation to the typology outlined above, perhaps ignoring the fourth, that of 'reflexive moral character'. Whether we need to say anything about *minimal* conscience in relation to Jesus may well depend, of course, on our judgement about his capacity to experience a *reactive* conscience. We begin, then, with the question whether Jesus could have known or experienced conscience in this sense. Could Jesus have known the experience of *guilt,* for example, for something he had done?

We have admitted that Jesus could have been *accused of* having no conscience, were his actions or words deemed to be immoral by his hearers, and not accompanied by obvious remorse. We take the assumption that Jesus was sinless; an assumption deeply rooted in Christian tradition. It is worth adding that this carries a further implicit assumption, that we accept certain implications of the concept of *sin:* some actions, for example, though not necessarily some *types* of action, are bad in a way which transcends human judgement upon them. Now, it might *appear* that if Jesus was sinless, he would never have known shame, guilt or remorse. It might *even* appear that he could never have known the *possibility* of these things, except by observation of the behaviour of his friends and his enemies.

It is actually not quite obvious that Jesus-as-sinless could never have known guilt or remorse. We are only too familiar with situations where we 'do the right thing' (have a baby vaccinated, for example) and the results of the action turn out badly. In such situations we might at least regret what we did, and may come to suppose that we acted wrongly. Did Lazarus suffer a lingering and painful second death after he was raised? We are, in any event, told that he was the subject of plots to kill him (John 12.10–11). Would Jesus have regretted his action in raising Lazarus, felt remorse, wondered if it might have been wrong?

Of course, by hypothesis, the action (the vaccination, for example) would be the right thing to have done, so the party concerned is *genuinely innocent*. If *results* or *outcome* were the standard by which our actions are to be judged, we would have to suppose that Jesus' sinlessness must have been based upon either an insight into the outcomes of his actions, or a trust in the guidance of someone (his Father) who *did* have such insight. Then there could never be any *cause* for regret or remorse. A more immediately appealing and less problematic approach would be to suggest that to regret one's action, undertaken in conformity with God's law, on the basis of its outcome is to show a less than wholehearted trust in God, a belief that the extent of my action constitutes a limitation upon God's sovereignty. Again, regret or remorse would be impossible, *this* time because they would themselves be ruled out by the presumption of sinlessness.

On either of these readings, it can be made to appear that Jesus never knew guilt for his own actions. An observer with perfect knowledge would find Jesus to be perfect, sinless. A human observer who might doubt the moral quality of some of his actions might nonetheless be impressed by his remarkable lack of expression of guilt or remorse, and might even be impressed enough to suggest that Jesus 'had no conscience'! That, though, is to hark back to the third-party use of this phrase rejected above.

An alternative approach to the question might be to return to the issue of whether there are alternative affective responses to actions of a *positive* kind which can be used to indicate the possession of reactive conscience. In the discussion of articulate conscience above we have noted that the rhetoric of conscience is often seen to provide a vocabulary for at least two kinds of judgement upon past (and perhaps anticipation of future) actions. One is *negative,* associated with prohibition and guilt. The other might be expected to be *positive,* but may in fact be simply 'not negative' – not quite the same thing. The pair of concepts used in Rom. 2.15 amount to 'accuse' (wrong) and something like 'excuse' or 'defend' (which might imply '*all* right', but certainly does not mean 'right-as-opposed-to-wrong'). What does *not* seem to be at issue is the concept of conscience as extended into the realm of *praise* or *adulation.* We have said that the primary phenomena of reactive conscience appear in sin and guilt. Yet if articulate conscience might permit a richer panoply of judgements, should we be so restrictive in our understanding of reactive conscience?

A matter of great relevance to what we might call 'positive uses' of the various senses of conscience is the theological evaluation of acts-beyond-duty. Are there acts which we may do *over and above* what is required of us, such that they may have (to use an ugly modern phrase) 'added value' and be *praised* accordingly? Famously, the fourteenth of the 39 Articles of the Church of England offer a horrified reaction to any such suggestion, smelling the intrusion of salvation by works.[20] Jesus' teaching that 'when you have done all the things which are commanded you, say 'we are unworthy slaves; we have done that which we ought to have done' (Luke 17.10) is called to mind to support such a position. There is, of course, a real and urgent question here, namely the relation of the moral life to the life of the saints, and the relation of the proper demands of God's *universally* valid law to His *particular* call on my life in ways which are quite local to my own service of Him. As suggested above, this is a continuing and unavoidable theme, whether it be under the language of general and special vocation, or of command (or precept) and counsel. In Jesus' case, it can have the appearance of a question whether Jesus knew some element of *self-satisfaction,* maybe no more than the capacity to step back and take self-conscious pleasure in a job well done and a life well lived.

One point at least might be made here. The 'capacity to step back', as I termed it, is precisely what is integral to the experience of *articulate* conscience. And it is *precisely* this capacity which is at issue in the life of Jesus, and in the judgement that conscience cannot be ultimate, but must be transcended. There is, of course, an entirely appropriate response to the life lived in perfect conformity with God's will, whether or not this is taken to transcend the demands of a 'general morality', and that is *joy*. This is not, of course, joy sought for its own sake, not really joy *sought* at all, in the obvious sense of that word. Jesus' life might well be held to constitute a kind of critique of the notion mentioned in a previous section, that there can be serviceable boundaries placed between the demands of 'morality' and response to the specific call of God. The 'Sermon on the Mount' and its parallels, often held up as a paradigm of moral teaching (though sometimes associated with unfortunate expressions such as 'impossible ideals'), might in a sense be taken to constitute an extreme critique of the safer and more protective pretensions of much supposed moral thinking, scaled as it is to the criterion of what can be 'reasonably expected'.

Doubts remain, though, given the apparent specificity of Jesus' vocation. The cross, which is after all the apparent horizon of Jesus' earthly life, is first of all hardly the place where we would look for *joy,* indeed perhaps the very last place. We may believe that Jesus would have wanted things to be otherwise, but his special vocation was set in the way of the cross. Or may it be that this is not really such a *special* vocation? The content of much moral theology constitutes, after all and at best, a kind of sustained reflection on what follows from the recognition that 'we have been crucified with Christ', that this, too, is our vocation, and forms a central element of our understanding of the meaning and purpose of baptism, a necessary prelude to participation in that resurrection life which is properly the goal of all our living.

It remains possible that the case of Jesus *is* in important senses different. Perhaps *for us* death to self is a kind of moral imperative, yet we believe that he did not face death gladly, or at least that he saw the possibility that things might have been otherwise, and requested that things might indeed be otherwise. Our dying has about it in a general way an inevitability which deprives it very greatly of the character of obedience, though the important continuing reflection on the theological significance of martyrdom constitutes a relevant strand of insight here.[21] Jesus' death to self has, indeed, a unique character. The very fact that he saw that 'things could have been otherwise' is, however, extremely important.

Did Jesus make moral judgements?

We note above that, for Thomas Aquinas, conscience is 'the mind of a person making moral judgements'. What is the relation between 'making moral judgements' and action? On one model, the process of 'moral thinking' might resolve itself into a range of possibilities of good or evil which it is then the task of will to decide upon. On such a view, the knowledge of both good and evil does not in itself determine that one will act for the good. Another different model integrates the process in such a way that the perception of good action and the performance of that action are related naturally; when the mind of a person makes a moral judgement the appropriate conclusion of the process will be the action which conforms to that judgement. The first model offers us a kind of conception of conscience as a 'moral faculty', with its detachment and isolation of the will from moral reason.[22] If this first model is to be conformable with what we might term moral sanctity at all, it will be because, once reason has discriminated the moral character of each possibility, the choice of will is *necessarily* restricted to those which are morally acceptable. In short, there is no *temptation* to do wrong, no *countenancing* of bad action. In the second model the discovery of good and the ruling out of bad action simply *constitutes* simultaneously a choosing; a choosing which may resolve, perhaps, on to a range of permissible alternatives. The discarded possibilities may, of course, carry a kind of illusory decontextualized capacity to be seen as good, but their good will only be good *in other circumstances*. When seen for what they are, here and now, they have no power to tempt the morally good person. They are not *genuine* alternatives for action.

We might ask, then: did Jesus ever make moral judgements? And if he *did,* what character did his making of moral judgements display? For example, did alternative possibilities for action exercise a control over him? The temptation narratives of the Gospels (Matt. 4.1–11, Mark 1.12–13, Luke 4.1–13[a] – John 6) constitute a *locus classicus* for exemplifying the assertion of the author of the Epistle to the Hebrews, that Jesus was 'tempted in all things as *[we are, yet]* without sin' (Heb. 4.15). It is, after all, a superficially puzzling thing that the sinless Jesus could be tempted. Does not authentic temptation actually betoken some lack, perhaps a lack of trust? This is an issue to which we need to turn when we come to examine the question of moral knowledge, and the Genesis narratives, below. It is, at least, worth remembering that *these* temptations are radically *externalized;* they are very far from being presented as cases of 'inner conflict'. There are other moments where we begin to see something of the context within which temptation may threaten; the demands of the crowds during times of extreme weariness, and the demands of the cross in the face of desire for life. May we hear in the words 'Father, if it be possible, let this cup pass from me...' (Matt. 29.39, Luke 22.42) a moment of temptation, an element of genuine 'internal' moral weakness? Yet even *without* the addition of 'Yet not as I will, but as you will' we may scarcely see in this the evidence of *actual* sin. Jesus' humanity is a humanity in which desire has its proper place (here, the desire for life, and to avoid suffering; emphatically *not* the fear of death or of its consequences), but that means *both* that he is able to *have* (good) desires, *and* permit them to be subordinated to the desires of his Father in their extreme specificity. He could wish things to *be* otherwise, but not wish to *do* otherwise than his Father's will.

The limits and criteria for 'moral thinking' thus presented appear to constitute, as we might expect, a desire to be conformable to the Father's will. Even were we also to recognise in Jesus' life some more indirect or intermediate principle of moral discernment,[23] the specific form of personal conformity is quite enough to suggest to us the genuine twin experiences of obedience and of the *possibility* of disobedience. How this relates to our own experience of 'making moral judgements' will depend in part on the principle or method of discernment which Jesus is seen to have used in his life. Those principles which he taught and commended appear to be, and to be presented as, a restatement and radicalization of the Law of Moses, appearing in specific circumstances as a relatively unremarkable casuistry of tradition.

We might indeed affirm, then, that Jesus made moral judgements. Whether we want to use this as a basis for answering the question whether Jesus had a conscience will depend on the extent to which we are impressed by the necessity of the possession of certain 'moral emotions' playing a characteristic role in conscience. If answering the question about the possession of conscience affirmatively implies that Jesus learnt criteria of action through the proper experience of *actual* guilt associated with personal wrongdoing, then a negative answer is inevitable. We may, however, have reason to hold that Jesus had 'the mind of a man which made moral judgements'; in *this* sense, yes, he had a conscience. This does not necessarily imply the ultimacy of conscience, though. The author of the Epistle to the Hebrews also speaks of Jesus' having been 'made perfect' (Heb. 5.9), a statement which may sound puzzling to readers accustomed to think of 'not perfect' as amounting to 'imperfect'. The claim which needs to be made at this point is that the process of being 'made perfect' implies precisely in one aspect a narrowing of practically conceivable options for action to those which genuinely conform to moral choice. Lack of conformity to the Father's will appears and becomes progressively less and less a truly available 'choice'. Our most characteristic experiences of the *making* of moral judgements are what come to be most obviously *reduced* in this transformation of character.

It may be helpful at this point in our investigation to introduce some recognition of the ways in which Christian tradition might contain elements sceptical about the value of 'moral knowledge'. This is obviously also worthwhile in that it offers a suitably quizzical comment upon the way in which slogans such as 'knowing the difference between right and wrong' have become part of the politico-moral debate in contemporary

Britain, and perhaps elsewhere. When there appear to be few or
no behavioural norms held by a sufficient number of people for
there to be any easy association of 'public standards' with
'objective morality', it appears that a kind of collapse into
subjective moral mysticism follows. It is unclear what is *gained*
by a radio reporter placing a microphone in front of a five-year-
old, asking 'Do you know the difference between right and
wrong?', whether or not the answer given is 'Yes'. Yet because
the richer conceptions of conscience, and especially what we
have termed 'articulate conscience', provoke us to examine
claims to moral knowledge, the theological status of such
matters needs to be raised.

The critique of moral knowledge

We have seen that 'articulate conscience' relates to the apprehension and application of moral truth; to self-conscious moral
knowledge, and the regulation of conduct. At this point, if not
earlier, a thought may occur to the theologically-inclined
reader. The creation narratives of the Old Testament, when
they use the expression 'knowledge of good and evil', do not
appear to do so in a positive way. Far from being scolded for
'not knowing the difference between right and wrong' (which,
superficially, is what 'knowledge of good and evil' may
appear to amount to) the first human couple are commanded
not to eat fruit which offers the potential for 'the knowledge
of good and evil'.

How should we regard this part of Scripture in relation to
our inquiry? This is not simply a general question about 'biblical authority'. It is a question about the way in which we are
to interpret the 'creation narratives'; as literal or semi-literal
history, as the 'history of Everyone' in a kind of mythico-
phenomenological sense, or in some other way. There are, as
any modestly sophisticated commentary will note, questions
relating to the layers of history of the narrative which ought
somehow to be brought into account, even if only by explicitly choosing to accept the 'text' as we have it before us.
There is an undeniable potential for the text to be read as the
record of an almost 'competitive' relationship between God

and his creatures. The role of God is to keep human beings in their place, and thereby protect his own position. There can, of course, be a quite innocent reading of this in which it serves human interest to *be* in proper relationship with God, and the disobedience both constitutes and inaugurates a breaking of right relationship. God is not, then, being self-interested *at the expense of* human interest. Yet there are elements in the narrative which might encourage a less favourable interpretation.

A further central question in assessing the significance of the narrative lies in a further kind of 'symmetry-problem'. Actually, there are probably a number of problems of symmetry implicit here, but the one I have most immediately in mind is forced upon us by the combination of the dual account of creation (Genesis 1–2.3; 2.4f), and the Christian doctrine of salvation. The first creation account is able to affirm that God was satisfied with His work of creation: 'God saw that it was good'. This is then associated with – immediately followed by – an independent creation narrative in which, apparently, the goodness of creation is upset by human disobedience of an explicit command of God, albeit motivated and in part perhaps mitigated by equally external factors in the shape of the serpent. It would be possible, perhaps, to read the first account as a sort of proleptic reassurance that God *will* make and see all things well, but this is hardly how the redactor who has given us our book of Genesis has seen the matter. It would also be possible to read the primitive goodness as usurped by human disobedience ('the Fall'), so that 'history' viewed as 'salvation history' becomes a drama of salvation-as-restoration. The primitive hope is the hope of a return to Eden, a divine or human-with-divine undoing of the disobedience which precisely counters the effects of the Fall.

Such a view is common, and may appear, at least superficially, to lie behind a great deal of Christian theology. The symmetrical vision is spectacularly displayed in certain elements of Edwin Muir's poem 'The Transfiguration' with its vision of a finally dis-crucified Christ.[24] This is not, I submit, a terribly comforting or theologically instructive vision. Jesus' image of the Kingdom of God appears to be a more positive basis of hope than a restoration or return, for all that it involves undoing the effects of human disobedience and transgression. Now, some caution is needed here. What is precisely *not* being contemplated is the replacement of a 'restoration' model of salvation with a naively 'progressivist' model of inevitable immanent historical achievement of the Kingdom of God. If the goal of creation is more than a return to the Eden pictured in Genesis chapters 2 and 3, then the 'progress' or advance implicit in that model is grounded theologically or not at all. It is hope in God, and not hope in the recuperative powers of a creation placed at arm's length from God, which is at stake here.

If it is appropriate to express distaste for a symmetrical model, by which salvation becomes a restoration of the situation of Eden, it is urgent that we ask after not only the meaning of the Genesis story as such, but also the way in which it may be seen to offer possibilities for its own transcendence. The task is to provide an account whereby the properly positive element of the Genesis narrative can be affirmed, pointing up the extent to which it contributes towards the proper and final outcome of creation. Investigation might be opened up on many fronts; for our own purpose, the major concern will be with the questions of moral *self-judgement* and *self-consciousness*.

It is worth noting that the so-called 'knowledge of good and evil' as it appears in many English translations of Genesis chapters 2 and 3 is misunderstood if the reader takes it as referring solely to a compartmentalized kind of knowledge called *moral* knowledge. The story of the Tower of Babel (Gen. 11.1–9) is in fact a continuation of the same theme, because the 'knowledge' is after a fashion *technological;* the knowledge of 'how to do things'. 'Good and evil' might with more justice, though greater awkwardness, be read as 'well and badly'. Does this *exclude* from consideration anything we might think of as moral knowledge? Not if we take the suggestion that anything which we would interpret narrowly as of 'moral' significance would be taken by the author to be relevant to the task of *living* well or badly, as a special form of 'technical' knowledge circumscribed by this particular objective. The *moral* then becomes just one element of a broader capacity to discern and make plans for change or alteration to things in general.[25]

If this is fair, it implies that the biblical author holds a quite organic conception of criteria for moral value, in common with much recent philosophical thinking on moral value. We should note one way in which the 'knowledge of good and evil' has results for the couple: they become aware of their nakedness. Whereas, previously, they were 'naked and not ashamed', the 'knowledge' which they have gained has included this much at least: the knowledge of their nakedness, and the motivation to cover themselves from each other, and to hide from God. There are, then, in this story the basis of reflections upon *both* consciousness *and* conscience. There cannot, of course, be any suggestion that the author imagines the couple to have been *unconscious,* or indeed completely bereft of anything which we would call 'knowledge', before their transgression. Most specifically, they have the very precise command not to eat the fruit, which one might imagine to constitute a particular instance of 'knowing good and evil', but this is known as a bare and externally imposed 'duty' rather than a genuine piece of significant knowledge. The serpent is able to question the results of a transgression in ways which constitute both a questioning of the specific declared *results,* or perhaps (to be more cautious) their *meaning* ('you shall not *die...*'), and also a raising of uncertainty in the woman which suggests a limitation on her knowledge of what the eating of the fruit precisely *does* signify (she does not know what she can do by eating the fruit, does not know *why* it was prohibited).

It is probably a mistake even to try to imagine in any great detail what kind of psychology or experience the author of this story imagined Adam and Eve to have before they ate of the fruit. The radical exteriorizing of both command and temptation is surely significant in a *negative* way: they do *not* eat out of curiosity, thinking 'I wonder what would happen if...' Freedom is given, but freedom circumscribed by a specific limit, which has to be explicitly stated. There is no narrative of internal struggle against the command, upon which the serpent is able to feed in his tempting of the woman. The significance of this absence is clear in the change which occurs after the eating; their nakedness, which was no occasion of shame in them before, now becomes a matter of extreme self-consciousness, so that they hide first from each other and then also from God. God was not, presumably, disturbed by their nakedness at earlier times, and the comment that they were *not* ashamed *then* is not offered to us by way of implication that they *should have been*. Eating the fruit has brought them a new capacity, a capacity to 'see things otherwise' than as they are. It leads towards the very essence of technological capacity which, as noted above, is contained within the 'knowledge of good and evil'.[26]

The deepest insight into human rebellion contained in these chapters is that of *independence,* rather than of *rivalry,* independence initially provoked from without, by 'the serpent'. It seems possible to say that one element of this independence lies precisely in the object of our investigation, namely in the possibility of conscience. If this claim can be substantiated, it ought at least to suggest something of the interest inherent in the question whether Jesus had or knew the experience of conscience. Conscience appears to connect with the capacity to *stand back* from the self and *reflect upon* one's actions, to be a judge of the self. There is, in effect, a twofold movement, self-consciousness and self-judgement, the second dependent upon the first. Genesis chapters 2 and 3 appears to imply some measure of negative judgement upon both of these.

In the next section we shall discuss further some of the more obvious objections to the claim that conscience *as such* can be seen as a bad thing. To anticipate briefly, the Christian doctrines of salvation and of redemption may be seen as offering more than a return to a kind of primitive naïveté, and the process of transcending conscience and inappropriate self-consciousness is not one which 'simply returns everything to where it was'. For the present, we need to note that the most basic element of the experience of the first human couple consequent upon their disobedience was a certain distancing of consciousness and the self, a capacity to see the self as an object of judgement and evaluation. This is not in itself an experience of guilt, which might be regarded as a traditional element of the 'inheritance of the first sin' when viewed historically and racially. It is, though, a necessary *element* in the phenomenology of guilt, and insofar as it constitutes a second voice of judgement upon the self *alongside* the judgement of God it offers a number of disturbing possibilities. One is, naturally enough, the possibility of a *false* judgement (that is, one at variance with God's). Another is the error of *priority* in judgement. For where is the individual to look *first* for truth in judgement? Should one trust in God's willingness unashamedly to confront us in our nakedness, in our complete transparency before him, or look first to our own judgement on our nakedness and act according to that judgement instead?

It is possible both to affirm the sinlessness of Jesus, and also to suggest that in this aspect at least Jesus was an 'inheritor of human fallenness'; he had the *capacity* for guilt, as an actual reality of reflexive self-awareness. Given that word 'inheritor', it ought to be admitted that the analysis offered may thus far be ambivalent between an 'individual' and an 'historico-racial' interpretation of the Fall. What *is* to be asserted quite explicitly is that Jesus does indeed, as the author of the Letter to the Hebrews asserts, share those crucial elements of human experience which make it possible for us to know both temptation and guilt. The theological justification for regarding this as properly 'racial' is in fact grounded in soteriology; for example, in the kind of reflections which Paul offers on the racial significance of Christ as 'second Adam' (Rom. 5.12–21).

The provisionality of conscience

In his careful reconstruction of Thomas Aquinas's understanding of practical reasoning, Daniel Westberg presents a diagrammatic outline of Thomas's theory of moral judgement, a simplified version of which appears below.[27] Under 'normal' circumstances, when called upon to act, there is little or no 'deliberation', or thinking through of what one ought to do when faced with this or that situation, at all. Occasionally there may be cases which require serious deliberative attention, but it is certainly not necessary to the right operation of practical reasoning that this should occur in every case.

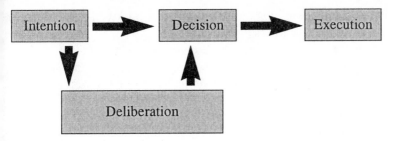

A careful modern reader of this theory may be inclined to say: but surely this is wrong. Each situation we encounter and which offers possibilities of action is, after all, unique. Should we not be prepared to deliberate in *all* cases, only relying on pre-established rules of action when deliberation is obviously impractical due to constraints of time or limited knowledge? Even when we *do* rely on established rules, we ought to do so self-consciously, not as a result of a sort of 'switching off' of moral reason, or idling along in a sort of moral 'neutral' with the gears disengaged. Responsibility can appear to demand this deliberative engagement.

The picture of much modern moral theory which this gives is a pretty fair one. Utilitarian forms of moral thinking illustrate it very well in the conflicts between 'rule' and 'act' forms of utilitarian evaluation of possible actions. Also any type of moral theory which discriminates absolutely between 'moral law' and the basis of contingent 'animal' desires, whilst simultaneously elevating the themes of freedom and responsibility, is likely to encourage a universal suspicion of motive and a desire for deep self-consciousness of moral or non-moral purpose in decision about action. It is a sign of the distinction of approach between 'classical' and 'modern' forms of moral thinking that the theme of radicalized conscious responsibility should have come to replace the ideal of 'naturalized' moral function.

It is no surprise that the instrument of much of this radicalization of responsibility is perceived to be 'conscience', viewed at times as almost supernatural in the urgency and inevitability of its demands. The nice irony here is that the more 'secular' the moral theory, the more elevated becomes the supernatural sense of the demands of conscience – as Kant

perhaps knew, in his recognition that, without actually constituting evidence for belief in God, or an argument for or proof
of God's existence, nonetheless the conscientious individual
will find himself in the experience of conscience standing
before a judgement which is self-interpreted as a divine
voice.[28] Theological moralists, too, have occasionally been
inclined to assert that conscience is precisely this, an immanent expression of the voice of God. This, however, can
readily invite confusion. It tends to concentrate attention upon
the question whether God ought to be obeyed (because
conscience is, by hypothesis, the voice of God). Yet much of
the literature on conscience is generated precisely by the
insight that the 'content' or 'dictates' of conscience are *not
unambiguously* (which is to say, *need not be 'heard' in
conformity to*) the voice of God, so that the question arises
whether and under what conditions conscience *ought* to be
listened to, be it (negatively) in ascribing guilt or (positively)
in guiding action. Whether the suspicion which directs our
concern be the one mentioned above, that God may not care
for us, or the different one that we may not be able to trust
ourselves to hear him correctly, we face uncertainty in giving
the 'voice' of conscience a role. Even in capitulating to the
apparent 'demands' of conscience we appear to be trusting in
our *own* resources of discrimination, or (if not that, then)
trusting in something which *may* be a simple projection of our
immediate desires, or of our fears, or the dictates and commitments of our culture.

The title of this essay signals a kind of attack upon
conscience, but it is not an attack which bids us to abandonment of the concept or the experiences associated with it. It
is, after all, plainly true that living between the twin possibilities of the hearing of the law as an external imposition, and
the receiving of the 'law written in our hearts', remains a
strong element of practical experience.[29] There is, of course,
a strong temptation to resent this gap, and to subordinate the
'otherness' of the call of moral law (whether it be mediated to
us through parenting, teaching, and preaching or through an
inner prompting which may be a memory of these things or a
divine 'voice', perhaps direct, perhaps mediated through some
'true nature of the self') to a life lived in accordance with

more immediately appealing goals. What would be good, we might think, would be to isolate areas of our lives where desire can be left to work its course quite innocently, and where the intrusions of 'conscience' can be dismissed as restrictions on properly Christian freedom.

There is, for example, a seductive strand of writing to be found in much modern theological reflection upon human sexual existence which might be regarded as 'anti-conscience' in this sense. It seeks to obviate, as far as possible, the need to reflect on the moral status of isolated and decontextualized acts, and in this it demonstrates a concern for which there is a venerable theological and philosophical tradition. One might, after all, hold that no act could be adequately characterized in such a way as to permit moral judgement to be passed upon it, unless it were to be specified in such an extremely precise way that only *this particular act* (whatever specific historical act is in question) was judged, and no commitment implied with respect to *any other* act. This extreme 'situationalism' is virtually impossible to characterize in any clear way, or at least impossible to characterize if its judgements are to connect with anything which might be termed moral *thinking*. Let us, though, leave such worries to one side, because, in practice, concern with the status of *types-of-act* can never be wholly absent as soon as situational reflection becomes confronted with human reality.

The thought, then, is that the particulars of our sexual existence as individuals can in general be trusted as an outcome of the creative intention of a loving God. As such, they are to be welcomed and cherished as a gift of His grace. Amongst the criteria for judging acts would be their conformity to these truths of our individual sexual characters. The reality of this 'simple trust' model is actually and obviously more complex. Because the 'sexual character' of some individuals appears to involve expression in the form of acts generally regarded as at best unfortunate – the involvement of children (whether apparently 'consenting' or not) and animals being obvious cases where our 'at best' is being stretched a bit thin – the defenders of a comfortable 'grace of sexual character' model find themselves forced to develop a typology of good and bad acts at one stage removed from a 'physical' characterization, but still adopting generic descriptions such as 'exploitative' or 'cruel' or 'harmful' (or on the positive side 'loving' or 'faithful'). It turns out, of course, that these act-type-descriptors quickly become practically unusable in the face of the impossibility of agreed and serious application. The process of moral abstraction which was meant to help us theologically has in fact transformed the business of moral analysis from analysis of acts to analysis of concepts; moral thinking has become unambiguously moral philosophy.[30]

It is clear that there is something right here, and also something horribly wrong. What is *right* is a belief in the possibility of a natural state in which simple trust and genuinely good action can be viewed as organically interdependent. As (in spite of certain apparent visionary passages to the contrary) no one really believes this to be possible without appropriate discrimination, this is also correctly perceived to be a *goal* and not a present *possession*. What is *wrong* is at its deepest the refusal to ground the conceptual basis of discrimination where it belongs. It properly belongs (as Roger White puts it, summarizing Barth's approach) 'in a resolute refusal to look elsewhere than to God's self-revelation to learn what He is like' – and, moreover, to learn from this the kind of character which can properly sustain our human living.[31]

One way, then, of expressing dissatisfaction with an easy 'grace of character' model is to remark that the model introduces a capacity to engage in a second trust; an immediate trust in 'character', and only secondarily a trust in God. As the aspects of character which may be trusted have been discriminated on the basis of ways of thinking which might themselves be questioned both methodologically and in their specific application, it is doubly clear that the basis of trust is something much more *mundane* than it is *theological*. It is, perhaps ironically, often those who (in sexual or ecological or whatever other areas of moral theology) want to promote holism and naturalism most strongly, and wish to assert the goodness of certain aspects of character and of those actions which flow naturally in conformity with them, that are *most* concerned with the necessity and ultimacy of moral *thinking* and moral *consciousness*. The creator and sustainer of their moral vision is a particular form of moral rationalism. Thus we see that a partial *resentment* of conscience can lead to a revitalised *commitment* to extreme forms of articulate conscience.

A further and obvious motivation to entrench conscience, and consciousness of moral deliberation, is the suggestion that human dignity requires *self*-legislation, whether that be in the form of subjective development of moral norms, or self-acceptance and imposition of laws grounded independently of the self. It could be argued that both approaches have their proper place in moral–theological reflection, though their usual form is quite specifically untheological. I take it that the motivation works as follows. It may be that there is an objective source of moral norms external to the self. Perhaps I might even have some sufficient access to the source of those norms, so that I never need doubt what it is that the objective moral norms would require of me in any moment. Still, it is surely (so the thought goes) a further question whether I actually *do* what is required. And this distancing of requirement and decision creates the inner space necessary to entrench conscience; the shall-I-shan't-I dialogue is a necessary element of what constitutes the human being as moral agent, and human dignity demands this. Without it we would be pure automata; or, if not that, then we would have placed ourselves unthinkingly (irresponsibly?) at the mercy of a source of moral norms over which we have no control.

Reflection upon these claims could detain us for a good while, but some brief comments upon them, taken as claims based around a theological interpretation of moral objectivity, will have to suffice. The first claim being made is that we can see what is right, and know it as such, but still have a *further* decision to make about whether to do it. This is, certainly, the process of 'detachment of will' around which much reflection upon conscience is based, and which was mentioned in the introduction to this investigation. Seriously to entertain this seems to betoken a lack of understanding of the claim which is being made, for how could one know what is *right* and entertain the possibility of not conforming to it? There does not seem to be the basis of a serious moral psychology here. Regarding the question of human dignity, that dignity is surely precisely the dignity of the human *creature,* and as such the desire to retain a space from which to judge the creator appears self-defeating. This self-defeating quality appears to be a straightforward deduction from the relationship of *creature* to *creator,* and the dependence even in the area of 'moral truth' which the creature thereby has. It is possible to support the requirement of conformity to that truth rhetorically by an appeal to God's power (as we find Peter Geach, or in a more immediately sympathetic way William Schweiker, doing),[32] or to his love, but in the end these are moves which belong more to the preaching of the evangelist than to the faith of the believer.

The discussion in this section of the essay has been designed to demonstrate the problems associated, on the one side, with attempts to take the transcending of conscience seriously as a *present* reality,[33] and on the other with a radical entrenching of conscience in a way designed to make it an *ultimately* positive part of human existence. In conclusion, we need to return to the possibility of an intermediate way, of the transcending of conscience as implicit in the process of sanctification. We note again the exteriority of both temptation and command experienced by both 'first' and 'second' Adam. We note, too, the natural desires of Jesus as exhibited in his expression of preference against the way of suffering; note also his willingness to conform to the will of his Father, not as the result of some general moral norm but even in the specific vocation of the cross. It is not simply a fragment of 'sacramental' practice which says to Christians that this way is theirs also; the call to work out our salvation, and the specificity of our own individual callings, is one which lies on the far side of the cross. Yet in our lives these two coexist beside each other, resurrection life and the life of the 'old nature'.

Did Jesus have a conscience? Jesus was, it appears, both intimately acquainted with the Law and also with the will of his Father for himself. He appears to have seen at crucial moments that things might be otherwise than the specifics of his Father's will might desire; and we have identified the capacity to 'see things otherwise' as crucial to a great deal of our authentic moral experience, and seen too the way in which it might be regarded as placing Jesus alongside us; he too was an 'inheritor' of this along with us. For the devil's temptations (or the crowd's) to *count* as temptations at all, we may suppose that capitulation was thinkable for him. The willing recognition of the authority of the Father does not, then, constitute a kind of episodic conformity, a discrete choice when each act of potential obedience presented itself to go along with the Father's desire – how might we be able to square our understanding with that of the Epistle to the Hebrews if it did? Rather, we see a *progressive* submission which is never not-submission. That this admits of being termed 'obedience' and that we can speak at all of 'submission' is to suggest that Jesus is indeed able to sympathize with us, and comprehend our experience of conscience in that of the 'minimal' conscience, conscience as the formation of moral character.

There is a sense in which the incarnation of Christ constitutes a fresh beginning, properly seen as 'second Adam'. Yet this should not be seen as 'second Adam restoring Eden'. The instability of Eden is seen, in the very fragility of its paradise; the Kingdom of God promises no such instability. The Christian affirmation is that Jesus' life does *more* than simply point the way towards the universal *potential* for submission to God's will to be so natural and intuitive in outline, the hearing of his will so unmistakable in its specificity, that the inner *struggle* of minimal conscience and even the inner *dialogue* of articulate conscience become a memory, or still less. The practical significance of this for the believer is seen in the context of the general theological question of the relation of the believer to Christ, to the Jesus who has shown the possibility of transcending conscience and submitting fully to the authority of the Father. About which, some things must be said in conclusion.

Firstly, the focus of much of this essay, and of the literature on conscience, is strongly influenced by concerns with the individual, and with behaviour in accordance with self-accepted norms, albeit interpreted as 'objective moral truths'. This does, of course, lend an aspect of concern with moral self-righteousness and purity-to-self to the whole discussion, and a concern with what is often called moral integrity. The extent to which this is a dangerous preoccupation has surely never been expressed with greater clarity than in Bonhoeffer's

Christocentric account of conscience,[34] where the threat of false unity and premature integrity is noted as an obvious danger, and the continuity of what he terms 'natural' conscience with conscience made free in Christ is also given serious weight. Yet, secondly, once it is admitted that the integrity which matters is unity with Christ, we recognise too that conscience becomes a properly ecclesiological notion, one which redraws the boundaries for recognition of authority in action and decision. The presumption of the ultimate judgement's belonging to *self* having been overturned, the twin questions of submission-and-authority, and discernment of truth, are played out in this new ecclesio-organic context of the body of Christ. We see in this the way in which the claims of conscience appear inevitably, from whatever source, to constrain us to look more closely at the depth of dysfunction which exists in that body. It might be remembered by those who have practical power effectively to *command* 'obedience' that the way of the cross might make demands of faithful *endurance* upon them as well, even at such points as the bearing of so-called 'conscientious objection'. Those who conscientiously object might, on the other hand, usefully reflect on various aspects of their stand, such as their capacity to be wrong, the variety of integrities which are at stake (of self, community, Church), and do so with appropriate humility. Conscience, whether reactive, minimal or articulate, can offer a perfectly appropriate vehicle for the practical expression of a variety of genuine forms of dis-integrity, forms which may actually *need* expressing. But because the dis-integrity of individual, Church and creation is not ultimate, conscience itself is not ultimate, and we may hope beyond the experience of it to a fulfilment in the one who is Truth himself.

Notes

1   Compare this with Luther's distinction between being able to 'do the good' and to 'fulfill the good'. 'For to do the good is not to go after lusts... but to fulfill the good is not to lust at all.' (Martin Luther, *Luther's Works*, American Edition Volume

25: Lectures on Romans (Concordia, Saint Louis, 1972), p. 342.)

2   There is a quite particular element of the language of conscience which might be mentioned as an aside, because it plays a very significant part in the modern rhetoric of conscience, and in its entrenchment as an absolutely indispensable element of moral 'consciousness'. It is that of the 'rights of conscience', which may appear to mean no more than the right of the individual to follow his or her own beliefs. If it *does* mean no more than this, it is, of course, absurd. What does the language of rights add to the observation that an individual can act on the basis of his beliefs, or at least try to? On the other hand, it seems sometimes to mean the right of an individual to *decide moral truth* for him or herself; if I am acting 'in accordance with my conscience', then no one has the right to prevent me from so acting. The simple claim that I am acting conscientiously is enough to convey a certain 'immunity from prosecution', perhaps exemption from legal and moral judgement. And to *this* there can be no right in any absolute sense, or existence in community would be impossible. If the claim is the more modest one that a certain class of conscientiously held moral beliefs and consequent actions are to be regarded as immune from interference, this may be because of one of the following: (a) a belief in moral 'subjectivism' (the criterion for moral truth lies within each individual); or (b) a belief that the value of 'autonomy', the capacity of the individual to be his or her own judge in moral questions, at the very least suggests the legitimacy of offering a 'space' within which the individual should be allowed to make moral error without interference. The second of these deserves respectful treatment, but the issues it raises (such as whether autonomy really is a central value for human existence, and how it is to be understood; and the potential for discerning a genuinely possible 'space' for the exercise of autonomy, usually debated under the labels of 'public' and 'private' morality) cannot be followed through fully in this investigation.

3   C. S. Lewis, *Studies in Words* (Cambridge University Press, Cambridge, 1962) pp. 181–213, at p. 182.

4   Timothy C. Potts, 'Conscience', *in* Norman Kretzmann, Anthony Kenny, Jan Pinborg (eds), *Cambridge History of Later Mediaeval Philosophy* (Cambridge University Press, Cambridge, 1982) pp. 687–704, at p. 696.

5   C. S. Lewis, *Studies in Words* (Cambridge University Press, Cambridge, 1962) p. 186.

6　　Lewis excuses himself from a trawl through the relevant material. C. S. Lewis, *Studies in Words* (Cambridge University Press, Cambridge, 1962) p. 194. The reference to Thomas at the foot of this page should direct the reader to Question 79 of the First Part of Thomas's *Summa Theologica,* rather than Question 69.

7　　Thomas Aquinas, *Summa Theologica* 1, q. 79, art. 13.

8　　Timothy C. Potts, 'Conscience', *in* Norman Kretzmann, Anthony Kenny, Jan Pinborg (eds), *Cambridge History of Later Mediaeval Philosophy* (Cambridge University Press, Cambridge, 1982) pp. 687–704. Jerome appears to suggest that conscience is never fully extinguished in anyone, and yet slightly later speaks of conscience being 'cast down' in the lives of some people, so that it 'loses its place'. These are apparently inconsistent, but when Jerome speaks of the inextinguishable conscience he uses the transliterated Greek word '*synteresis*', whilst when he speaks of the conscience which may apparently be lost he uses the Latin '*conscientia*'. It is probably unlikely that any significance is intended by this distinction, but Jerome's readers inclined to the view that two different senses must have been intended.

9　　Thomas Aquinas, *Quaestiones Disputatae: De Veritate,* q. 16, 17; especially 16, art. 2; 17 art. 2.

10　Germain Grisez, *The Way of the Lord Jesus, I: Christian Moral Principles* (Franciscan Herald Press, Chicago, 1983) pp. 73–96, at pp. 73–75, 89–90.

11　Germain Grisez, *The Way of the Lord Jesus, I: Christian Moral Principles* (Franciscan Herald Press, Chicago, 1983) p. 79.

12　It may be noted that we have here a second sense of 'bad conscience', namely, a conscience which is a morally incompetent judge.

13　The central question of individual and corporate interest (and the priority of the human in 'corporate' interest) is, of course, a matter of real philosophical concern and interest. Because, theologically speaking, all interest rightly perceived is God's, the question of the unity of perception of interest and moral value is offered a particular 'frame' even if, in practical moral theology, the questions appear indistinguishable from their equivalents in a theory of potentially ultimate competition of interest. We cannot pursue the matter here beyond noting the extremely fast and unwarranted move which John Stuart Mill makes (*Utilitarianism*, chapter 4) from individual interest to corporate interest as a warning to those who would approach the question with insufficient caution. (Mill's claim is 'that each person's happiness is a good to that person, and the general happiness, *therefore,* a good to the aggregate of all persons'. The emphasis is mine.)

14 Joseph Fletcher, *Situation Ethics* (SCM Press, London, 1966).

15 Simon Blackburn, *Oxford Dictionary of Philosophy* (Oxford University Press, Oxford, 1994) p. 164

16 New American Standard Bible translation.

17 I suspect that it is partly concerns with the 'articulacy' of conscience which lead to Ronald Preston's concern that 'There has... been a tendency in 20th-century Continental Protestant theology to interpret conscience only in a negative sense'. See his article 'Conscience' in John Macquarrie and James Childress (eds.), *New Dictionary of Christian Ethics* (SCM Press, London, 1986), p. 118.

18 Arthur Miller, *Timebends* (Methuen, London, 1987) p. 426.

19 It is worth reflecting on two possible responses. First from the adulterer, who overhears the assertion that he has no conscience: 'Of course I do, but what I'm doing is perfectly all right.' I suspect that this would not affect the original judgement of lack-of-conscience; it might even be entrenched. On the other hand, another observer might agree that the infidelity is despicable, but respond to the assertion of 'no conscience' by saying something like 'but he's so kind to his children'. Which is to say, presumably, that he's not *all* bad, that he must have *some* conscience. This reinforces the suggestion that this kind of attribution to someone of the property of 'no-conscience' is a judgement on their (degree of) conformity to accepted social norms.

20 The Articles can be found in the *Book of Common Prayer*. The fourteenth Article reads: 'Voluntary Works besides, over and above God's commandments, which they call Works of Supererogation, cannot be taught without arrogancy and impiety: for by them men do declare, that they do not only render unto God as much as they are bound to do, but that they do more for his sake, than of bounden duty is required: whereas Christ saith plainly, When ye have done all that are commanded to you, say, We are unprofitable servants.'

21 For example Pope John Paul II, Encyclical Letter *'Veritatis Splendor'* (1993). Text and commentary contained in John Wilkins (ed.), *Understanding Veritatis Splendor* (SPCK, London, 1994). See pp. 158–161, sections 90–94.

22 There is not space in this essay to expound and attack the conception of conscience as a mental faculty. Something of what

is involved in holding such a view may be grasped by re-reading Thomas's definition of conscience, not as 'the mind of a man making moral judgements', but as 'the *part* of a man's mind which makes moral judgements'. These are obviously very different conceptions. This 'faculty-conception', and faculty conceptions of mind in more general ways (such as Descartes' understanding of the faculty-separation of the functions of intellect and will in the fourth of his 'Meditations'), render the giving of an adequate integrated account of moral psychology or mental experience more generally deeply problematic, for all that they are presented in order to *solve* certain problems in precisely such accounts.

23   Such as knowing the Father's will through the Mosaic Law.

24   'The Transfiguration' in Edwin Muir, *Collected Poems* (Faber & Faber, London, 1960) pp. 198–200. Muir clearly believes that this vision is of an irreversible state (see, for example, the closing lines, on the betrayal of Christ: 'Be quite undone and never more be done'). The basis of this apparently reassuring vision is unclear, however.

25   See further N. P. Williams, *The Ideas of the Fall and of Original Sin* (Longmans, Green & Company, London, 1927) pp. 39–51, especially p. 43f.

26   We might note the judgement of N. P. Williams, *The Ideas of the Fall and of Original Sin* (Longmans, Green & Company, London, 1927) p. 50: 'It would seem that, for J's sombre philosophy of history, civilisation and culture are, on the whole, a disastrous mistake'.

27   Daniel Westberg, *Right Practical Reason* (Oxford University Press, Oxford, 1994) p. 131.

28   Immanuel Kant, *The Metaphysics of Morals,* trans. Mary Gregor (Cambridge University Press, Cambridge, 1991) pp. 233–235.

29   I take it that the 'law written on their heart' (Jer. 31.33) is something more than a kind of corporate photographic memory of the written pages of the law. As the 'heart' is the symbol of the moral centre of the human person in the Old Testament, the place where parallels to our discussion of 'conscience' are referred, so the law written on the heart should presumably be heard as a natural predisposition and predilection towards the doing of the law. It is noteworthy that here the people appear to have a single 'heart'.

30   If 'traditional Christian teaching' is correct, a community which exhibited the truth of the law written on the heart would unself-

consciously restrict the range of possible forms of sexual existence which they might believe open to themselves to those of marriage and celibacy. Within these 'forms' there would be proper room for distinct hopes and desires, and also for the subordination of those hopes and desires to the will of God in its particularity. A married couple in the happy position of having the law within them might be trusted to explore the bounds of physical sexual encounter each with the other without either fear of harm, or fear of qualm.

31 See Roger M. White, 'Notes on analogical predication and speaking about God' in Brian Hebblethwaite and Stewart Sutherland (eds), *The Philosophical Frontiers of Christian Theology: Essays presented to Donald MacKinnon* (Cambridge University Press, Cambridge, 1982) pp. 197–226, at p. 224.

32 Peter Geach, *God and the Soul* (Routledge & Kegan Paul, London, 1969) p. 126f.; William Schweiker, *Responsibility and Christian Ethics* (Cambridge University Press, Cambridge, 1995) pp. 178–181.

33 On this point, an exposition of Paul's First Epistle to the Corinthians might have done just as well.

34 Dietrich Bonhoeffer, *Ethics,* trans. Neville Horton Smith (SCM Press, London, 1955) pp. 242–248.

3

Conscience in the Roman Catholic Tradition

Jayne Hoose

Introduction

Whilst many looking from the outside may see the Roman Catholic view of conscience as monolithic, based upon the view of the *Magisterium*[1] and derived from natural law, in practice, this perception is far from the truth and the complete picture is much more complex. Contemporary Roman Catholic scholars along with those from other denominations now acknowledge the need to consider a wide range of sources in the development of moral theology. These include not only natural law and official church teaching but also an increasing use of Scripture, the insights of a wide range of philosophers, past and present theologians and the wider church community including, for example, psychologists. Inevitably tensions result from different interpretations of the various sources of Roman Catholic moral theology. Many moral theologians thus find themselves in disagreement with the viewpoint expressed in documents emanating from the Vatican and with viewpoints expressed by other moral theologians.

Claimed foundations: Scripture and the early writers

Old Testament

There is little reference in the Old Testament to the Hebrew and Greek concepts for our word 'conscience'. The only clear reference to the way we use the word appears in Wis. 17. 11, which indicates the unquiet or bad conscience. The biblical vision of the 'heart', however, to which there are many references in the Old Testament, provides us with further insight. 'For the Semites, the heart was the seat of thoughts, desires and emotions, and also of moral judgement'[2].

Whilst there is nothing on 'antecedent' and 'following' conscience in the Old Testament it is clear that the heart can do more than just accuse following a wrong act, it can also listen to God (Isa. 51.7) and guide towards righteousness (Ps. 119.11). This profound vision of the heart, touched and moved by the Spirit, is seen as overcoming all extrinsic morality. God's Spirit is seen as providing an inner disposition towards and a call to do good and avoid evil (1 Kings 3.9). God writes his law in a person's heart, in their innermost being (Jer. 31.29-34, Ezek. 14. 1-3 and 36.26), thereby establishing a new covenant not only within the individual but with the entire community of Israel.

New Testament

The New Testament needs to be viewed in the context of the Old Testament which it came to fulfil, the message being that God will take away the heart hardened by sin and give a new or enlivened heart. God's calling, resounding in an individual's heart, is seen as both a religious experience and an experience of conscience. It is always marked by wholeness, the calling of the whole person. This is the law of love of God and of neighbour that is written on human hearts.[3]

The word 'conscience' appears 30 times in the New Testament, of which 15 are found in Pauline letters. Paul's use of this word has therefore received considerable attention from biblical scholars.[4] He uses the key concept of Stoic ethics, *syneidesis*,[5] which he fortifies with the biblical tradition of the 'heart' and further enriches with the dynamic presence of the divine Pneuma (2 Cor. 1.12, 4.1–2 & 5.11).[6] Many scholars (Willis,[7] Deidun,[8] Furnish,[9] Mahoney) appear to agree that Paul viewed conscience as a faculty possessed by all individuals, the faculty by which they evaluate the moral worth of their behaviour in the light of their beliefs.[10] It is, also, increasingly agreed (Davies[11], Thrall, Sevenster[12]) that Paul sees it not just as a retrospective faculty but as having a role in making decisions in advance of an action. Paul also uses *syneidesis* for the conscience that both accuses and defends the individual:

> When Gentiles, who do not possess the written law, carry out its precepts by the light of nature, then although they have no law, they are their own law, for they display the effects of the law inscribed on their hearts. Their conscience is called as a witness, and their own thoughts argue the case on either side against them or for them (Rom. 2. 14–15).

In addition, various conclusions which are open to dispute are drawn by some Roman Catholic theologians from two of the key passages relating to conscience in Paul's writings, 1 Cor. 8.7–13 and 10.23–30. Mahoney, for instance, holds that, within these passages, Paul indicates that individuals acting in accordance with their conscience would stand by their inner convictions, whilst not imposing their actions and convictions upon others, or criticizing those whose convictions and actions differ. In developing upon work by Delhaye,[13] Mahoney sees Paul strongly affirming the subjective aspect of conscience as a norm for behaviour, the force being derived from the individual's personal perceptions of morality, and the objective reality of God and his expectations of human beings. These expectations are not found simply in the formal legislation of God presented externally to the individual within the community, but are an internal source involving reflection on the law and an element of personal discovery.[14] For Häring, this does not mean that a good conscience is a matter of self-assurance and self-affirmation. Believers stand before God, who is their divine Judge and Saviour (1 Cor. 4.4), and do not make a judgement of conscience individualistically. They will instead seek the reciprocity of consciences (a concept further developed later in this chapter), being ever concerned for the integrity of the conscience of others (1 Cor. 10.25-29). All this, he says, fits with Paul's assertion that the word of mutual law is inscribed in our 'hearts' (consciences).[15]

According to Deidun,[16] however, Paul does not see conscience as the 'ultimate authority in moral judgement'. Otherwise he would not have intervened to correct the conduct of the 'strong' in 1 Cor. 8.12 and Rom. 14.15, whom one can assume would have been following their own consciences. In addition, other biblical scholars, including Sampley[17] and Furnish, hold that Paul 'never establishes conscience as a firm principle or guide to moral action'.[18] Maurer and Horsley point back to the origin of *syneidesis* as 'to know with (myself)' – the inner consciousness or awareness –, what Pierce sees as the non-moral usage,[19] suggesting that this may have been how the Corinthians used the term. Thus those who were described as 'weak' in *syneidesis* were perhaps merely unaware (or lacking in knowledge) of the truth regarding idols and idol meat (1 Cor. 8.7).

White[20] disagrees and refers to Lillie's[21] acknowledgement that, whilst conscience in Paul only refers to the pain of reflecting upon a wrong which has been committed, there is within that pain a judgement of right and wrong. He supports this with H. W. Robinson who shows:

> that in Pauline psychology *mind* in its good sense is that which comprehends the law of God, delights in it, and approves of it (Romans 7.23,25); while *conscience* includes a sense of rectitude, the appeal to moral judgement in others and the faculty for moral judgement in oneself – though this may become defiled (11 Cor. 8.7). Conscience is not for Paul, a source of ethical knowledge: it exercises judgement on the moral quality of acts after they have been committed. This as we have seen, does however imply learning from experience.[22]

Early writers

Whilst there is much agreement among scholastics regarding conscience as the unique and most relevant inborn disposition which makes human moral beings, scholastic theology and later moral theology are strongly influenced by the distinction between *syneidesis* (*conscientia*[23]) and *synteresis*.[24, 25]

Syneidesis was seen as the judgement or act by which a conclusion is reached that some particular thing or action is good or evil, whereas *synteresis* – the scholastics' *synderesis* – is the permanent capacity that urges human beings to do good and avoid evil, in the light of which they make their judgements.[26] [27]

A key concept within the work of Thomas Aquinas was practical intellect. Aquinas saw *synteresis* as an inborn disposition (*primus habitus*) towards the good, based upon practical moral reason which informs the individual that the good has to be done. The judgement of conscience, on the other hand, is a concrete moral judgement from the *synteresis* about what is good in a particular case:

> There is in the soul a natural habit of first principles of action, which are the universal principles of natural law. This habit pertains to synderesis. This habit exists in no other power than reason... The name *conscience* means the application of knowledge to something...[28]

Häring points out, however, that Aquinas did not, as was the case with the later Thomists, see this in a merely intellectual sense and ignore the uniqueness of a person and the depth of that person's heart. He placed emphasis on knowledge of the good, but, in so doing, used the biblical understanding of 'knowing', that is, knowledge from the depth of the heart. He saw the natural inclination of the will being bound up with the knowledge of practical reason, the will having a profound disposition to press towards the good as known by reason. For Aquinas right moral reasoning required the virtue of prudence, a sincere judgement of conscience occurring as a result of the inborn disposition, *synteresis,* and the virtue of prudence which, for its very being and function, presupposes a basic orientation towards the good.[29]

St Bonaventure and many others place their emphasis on the inborn disposition of the will, *synteresis* being the inborn disposition of the will to love and to desire what is good.[30] [31] The religious depth of this theory is found in the will being seen as touched by God, touched by divine love. Bonaventure, nevertheless, did not intend to devalue the intellect. The will was not seen as a blind force, but as a power drawn to known good. Right reason receives its dynamic force from the inborn disposition to love and to do what is understood in a particular instant as the good.[32] Portrayed in this way, as identified by Häring these schools do not appear to be as antagonistic as they are usually portrayed, but complement each other. They reach the same vision from different angles[33].

Natural law

From Scripture and the early writers, then, the Roman Catholic tradition derives its understanding of conscience as including the central core of the person, the awareness that one should do good and avoid evil and the faculty to work out what is right and what is wrong. The methodology applied within the Roman Catholic tradition in determining right and wrong is, however, based upon natural law, the approach to which employed by the *Magisterium* relies heavily upon the teaching of Thomas Aquinas. Aquinas appeared to accept two interpretations of natural law, one, influenced by the Stoics and Ulpian, which emphasizes the physical and biological structure of nature as the basis for morality, and the second, influenced by Aristotle, Cicero, and Gaius, which is centred around the capacity of human beings to discover through experience what befits human well-being.[34]

In the *Summa Theologiae* (1–2, qq.90–7) natural law 'is linked with the notion of law in general as an ordinance of practical reason (q.90), and with eternal law, which is the way of saying that God is the ultimate source of moral value and moral obligation (q.93)'.[35] Natural law is therefore seen as the human way of knowing the moral norms required and enabled by God, this knowledge being achieved by reflecting upon nature, that is, reflecting upon what it means to be fully human.[36] Humans achieve such reflection through the use of reason, whereas animals participate in God's law through instinct, reason being that which distinguishes human beings from everything else. Gula notes that 'reason' is not used here in the narrow sense of logic or analysis. Aquinas's sense of reason, *recta ratio,* involves the whole of the human tendency to want to know the whole of reality and come to truth. This, Gula says, includes research and observation, intuition, affection, common sense, and an aesthetic sense. Any sources which help our understanding of human nature are, therefore, appropriate for a natural law approach to morality.[37] Whilst it might be said that this shows Aquinas' preference to follow the 'order of reason' interpretation of natural law, he is not consistent in that he also retains Ulpian's 'order of nature' definition.[38]

This leaves the problem of whether or not there is one precept to natural law or several. For Aquinas there is one fundamental norm of natural law followed by more specific norms. The fundamental norm is to do good and avoid evil, good being that which allows the full realization of the human potential, and evil being that which prevents or inhibits such realization.[39] This, however, only provides a model for action, it does not help us to identify what is right or wrong. It is the specific norms arising from natural inclinations which allow concrete conclusions – practical reason perceiving the natural inclinations in the form of moral imperatives.

Aquinas identifies three basic inclinations to the good. The first is arrived at by asking what humans have in common with everything else that exists. Aquinas responds: the instinct to survive. From this natural law arrives at the first value of respecting life, from which Aquinas develops his arguments against suicide and in favour of killing in self-defence. More recent debates within the area of just war and the field of medical ethics offer other examples which draw upon this.

The second inclination is identified by asking what humans have in common with other animals, the answer being, the instinct for survival of the species – procreation and the education of offspring. This is the 'order of nature' strain of natural law in Aquinas and it is to this that he appeals when discussing sexual ethics.

The third inclination to the good is arrived at by answering the question, what do humans have which is specific to them? Aquinas identifies reason as being specific to human beings, the third inclination being to act rationally and follow one's reason. Aquinas then goes on to ask why we are given reason, responding that this is in order to discover truth and to discover it together within a social existence.[40] This is clearly the 'order of reason' strain of natural law and relates directly

to Aquinas' primary definition of natural law as human participation in eternal law through the use of reason. Aquinas
appeals to the order of reason of 'specific natural law' in relation to matters of justice. The Roman Catholic Church has
appealed to it in its development of social ethics.

The 'order of nature' interpretation emphasizes the physical
over the personal. In determining morality it tends to emphasize, and even absolutize, the physical and biological person
independently of reason and freedom. Personalism which
extends beyond the physical and biological to include the
social, spiritual and psychological dimensions of the human
person is very much secondary to physicalism. The physical-
ists' interpretation of natural law suggests a 'blueprint' theory,
God's will being written in nature – the rule of God and the
rule of nature, therefore, being one. Moral norms can, hence,
be determined by identifying what is needed for nature to
fulfil its purpose. In Catholicism this has been applied not just
at the level of person but also with respect to different organs.
The reproductive system, for instance, is seen as having the
purpose of procreation. It is in the areas of sexual and medical
ethics, and in particular with respect to reproduction, that this
interpretation of natural law has been dominant in Roman
Catholic teaching. The 'order of nature' has been seen as
being dominant over the 'order of reason' because it is derived
directly from God as opposed to directly from the person.
This view, however, clearly has its problems; if actions
against nature were more serious than those against reason we
would have to conclude, for example, that masturbation is
more serious than rape or incest.

Many contemporary theologians, including Curran[41] and
Rahner[42], see nature not as a fixed product, but as one which is
evolving. Moreover, human reason and freedom can intervene
within the limits of the physical laws to provide unexpected
circumstances. From this viewpoint nature is not prescriptive
and we discover what natural law requires by using reason to
reflect upon human experience. Whilst there is a strength in
recognizing the biological structure and function of human
nature in physicalism, this should not be confused with the
whole of human nature. Such an approach ignores the creative
capacities of the human person and sees human nature as static,

as opposed to changeable and developmental. There is increasingly a call for Roman Catholic moral theology to take seriously experience, history, change and development, a call to re-address the broader understanding of reason, *recta ratio*, identified by Aquinas. Such an interpretation of natural law differentiates between animals and humans, animals being subject to the order of nature and humans being provided by nature with what is necessary to realize their full potential. Natural order and moral order are, therefore, not the same, and humans can intervene, directing nature in a way that is properly proportionate to human moral development.

This has clear implications for the understanding of morality, morality based on natural law still being objective in that it arises from an informed effort to understand human reality in its totality and not from self-interest. We can, however, only grasp part of that reality at any one moment and our knowledge of what it means to be human continues to develop. Moral standpoints must, therefore, be open to change as our knowledge and understanding develop. The difference in individual capacities influenced by emotional and cultural conditions which affect the individual's perspective on reality must also be recognized. The Roman Catholic Church seems prepared to accept this with respect to social teaching, as seen in the American bishops' pastoral letter on war and peace, *Challenge for Peace* (1983): 'On complex social questions, the Church expects a certain diversity of views even though all hold the same universal moral principles'.[43] There are clearly, however, two methods of interpretation of natural law being applied today in official Catholic moral teaching, social ethics accepting the 'order of reason' interpretation whilst sexual ethics is based more, although perhaps not exclusively, on the 'order of nature' interpretation.

Morality based on natural law is nevertheless opposed to extreme forms of situation ethics. It is also opposed to voluntarism where the legislator determines right and wrong through their own will. Catholic teaching indeed claims that because morality is grounded in reality some actions can be judged to be right and some wrong. Catholic natural law teaching is also found to be in direct opposition to a divine command theory of ethics, knowledge of right and wrong being available to anyone prepared to reflect upon human experience to find truth, as opposed to relying on divine revelation. It is because of this that the Roman Catholic Church claims its teaching to be relevant to all, not just those of religious insight or motivation.

In summary, the Roman Catholic revisionists' view of natural law is based upon realism which involves neither blind obedience to positive law nor going one's own way. It involves discovering and seeking to do what is good by critically reflecting on all that it means to be human and all the relationships that it involves. The morality derived should, therefore, reflect the collective experience of what assists the human person in fulfilling their potential to be fully human. This means moral theology paying attention to both past and present experience. It must also be noted that, whilst consequences do not form the whole of moral reality, they cannot be ignored. The traditional natural law approach adopted by the *Magisterium*, in particular when interpreted with respect to the 'order of nature' has been criticized for taking a static view of natural law and not taking into account the possibility of change and development. What may have been positive for the flourishing of individuals in the past may not now be positive. The claims of an unbroken tradition of teaching by the Roman Catholic Church, despite what appear to be obvious changes regarding slavery, usury, religious liberty and the burning and torture of heretics (further details of which are provided later in this chapter), seemingly seek to deny this.

Recent developments – official teaching

The *Magisterium* of the Roman Catholic Church issues teaching statements in the area of 'faith and morals',[44] a number of which provide interpretation of the above roots in relation to conscience.

The Second Vatican Council

Vatican II contains what is usually regarded as the principal conciliar text, issued by the *Magisterium* of the Roman

Catholic Church, on conscience: paragraph 16 of the 'Pastoral Constitution on the Church in the Modern World', *Gaudium et Spes*. The following statement is possibly the most widely quoted, probably due to the clear implications it has for the dignity and respect of the individual conscience: 'His conscience is man's most secret core and sanctuary. There he is alone with God whose voice echoes in his depths.' Paragraph 16, however, contains much more than this, developing, in particular, a number of key scriptural themes. Each person is seen as having God's law inscribed on their heart, a law which is detected deep within a person's conscience, and a law which is not self imposed but must be obeyed. It is this law which calls a person to love good and avoid evil and which may at any given moment tell a person to do this or avoid that. A person's dignity is found in observing this law, which is fulfilled through the love of God and of neighbour, and is the law by which they will be judged.

It is the conscience which makes known this law and, in being obedient to their conscience, Christians are joined with others in the search for truth. Individuals and groups are seen to be increasingly guided by objective moral standards the more a correct conscience prevails.[45] *Gaudium et Spes* clearly emphasises the importance of the reciprocity of conscience and the inviolable dignity and freedom of the individual conscience. This is reiterated in the Declaration of Religious Liberty, para 3 of Vatican II:

> The search for truth, however, must be carried out in a manner that is appropriate to the dignity of the human person and his social nature, namely by free enquiry with the help of teaching or instruction, communication and dialogue. It is by these means that men share with each other the truth that they have discovered, or think they have discovered, in such a way that they help one another in the search for truth. Moreover, it is by personal assent that men must adhere to the truth they have discovered.
>
> It is through his conscience that man sees and recognizes the demands of the divine law. He is bound to follow his conscience faithfully in all his activity so that he may come to God, who is his last end. Therefore he must not be forced to act contrary to his conscience. Nor must he be prevented from acting according to his conscience, especially in religious matters.[46]

A number of more recent official texts also address issues of conscience, but seem to give greater priority to written law, and submitting to the *Magisterium* and its interpretation of the law. One of the more notable of these documents is the encyclical letter of Pope John Paul II, *Veritatis Splendor*.

Veritatis Splendor

Veritatis Splendor starts with the story of Jesus and the rich young man, weaving into the consideration of the dialogue in this passage Aquinas's classic definition of 'natural law' as 'nothing other than the light of understanding infused in us by God, whereby we understand what must be done and what must be avoided' (*VS* 12), and presenting the commandments not as a 'minimum limit' but as 'the first necessary step on the journey to freedom' (*VS* 15, 13).[47] The encyclical, however, then clearly goes on to place the emphasis upon Jesus as a teacher promulgating commands, authority being placed in these commands as opposed to Jesus himself. The second chapter, whilst concentrating on natural law methodology, moves over to a definition of natural law based on 'a kind of code, a manual of law, "laying down" (*VS* 50), often in great detail what should and should not be done'.[48]

Harvey sees here a 'grossly anachronistic portrayal of Jesus as a proponent of exceptionless moral norms'. He is deeply critical of the encyclical seemingly suggesting that there is a comfortable fit between the Decalogue, the law of Christ and the natural law. He points to the Decalogue as part of the Torah 'to some extent definitive of the relation between the people of Israel and their God' and advocating 'a range of responses to the Israelites' particular experience of the Lord's redeeming activity'.[49] He continues by highlighting Jesus' teaching as leaving the 'old law' behind, as exemplified by his healing on the Sabbath and his contradicting in various ways the command to honour parents. Harvey, indeed, notes that there seems to be no sign of concern for moral norms in Christ's teaching. He then supports these arguments by pointing to Paul's more drastic reinterpretation of the Law, citing two examples and parallelling them with apparently contradictory statements from the encyclical:

> We acknowledge that what makes a man righteous is not obedi-
> ence to the law, but faith in Jesus Christ ... I cannot bring myself
> to give up God's gift: if the Law can justify us there is no point
> in the death of Christ (Gal. 2.16, 21).

> In fact, human freedom finds its authentic and complete fulfilment
> precisely in the acceptance of the moral law given by God. God,
> who alone is good, and by virtue of his very love proposes this
> good to man in the commandments (*VS* 35).

> "All things are lawful" but not all things are helpful. "All things
> are lawful", but not all things build up (1 Cor. 10.23).

> By submitting to the common law, our acts build up the true
> communion of persons and, by God's grace, practise charity (*VS*
> 51).

Finally, Harvey points out that natural law does not rely on
theocratic ideas of redemption or conversion and, in its
discourse, is in stark contrast to the Decalogue and the law of
Christ. Trying to make it fit comfortably with them, therefore,
he sees as removing all creativity from the encounter.
Interestingly, moreover, the Pope does object in *Veritatis
Splendor* to the creative conscience, a caution which Harvey
clearly would see as invalid. Harvey sees the drawing together
of the Decalogue, the law of Christ and the natural law as
simply a bid to defend a univocal concept of exceptionless law
which does not exist.[50] With Lash he sees these 'exceptionless
moral laws' as a modern misinterpretation of a biblical, theological and moral tradition which does not recognize them.
    Lash also criticizes the apparent misrepresentation of
Aquinas as displaying a deeper interest in and a more simplis-
tic and monolithic understanding of the law than St. Thomas
actually had. Drawing upon Herbert McCabe, he points out
that Aquinas focused more upon dispositions, patterns and
habits of behaviour, individual and social, which issue in acts
and are grounded in norms, rather than on 'norms' and 'acts'.
Aquinas did not work out his ethics primarily in terms of the
'law'.
    There seems to be an emphasis within *Veritatis Splendor* on
the suppression of conscience and a move of power towards
the *Magisterium*. This appears to arise from a concern about
a strong link between freedom and subjectivity, a concern that

the all-important issue may be seen as following one's conscience at any given moment without there necessarily being any genuine intellectual or imaginative[51] pursuit of the truth. Whilst still recognizing that it is always right to obey one's conscience, the Pope insists that this should not involve submitting to subjective certainties but should always be based on a constant attempt to deepen the awareness of conscience regarding truth. That much is accepted by most writers. What is problematic is that, if one adopted the teaching of *Veritatis Splendor* the result for a Christian of such a search would mean not only submitting to the truth that is 'the new law' of the gospel, but submitting to the particular way in which it is interpreted by the *Magisterium*. This seems to be a departure from the teaching of Vatican II where we find recognition of the need for free enquiry *helped* by teaching or instruction, communication and dialogue.

This position is particularly problematic given the increasingly restrictive sense in which the term *magisterium* is being used. The word *magisterium* means the office or function of teaching. There are many within the church who exercise a true teaching function including catechists, religious educators, preachers and theologians. The term *Magisterium* has, however, recently been used within the Roman Catholic Church in a more restrictive sense to mean the teaching of the pope, and the pope himself in consultation with the bishops. Moreover, in *Veritatis Splendor,* as identified by Preston, its meaning is yet further restricted to the pope and his advisors (not the bishops as a whole, the encyclical being addressed to the bishops).[52] Such an understanding cannot be supported either theologically or historically. Christ is the Teacher, teaching being a part of his mission and a part he gave to the whole church. This does not deny the need for instruction within the Christian community, but the gifts of all members must be recognized and respected. Historically many of the Teachers of the Church (*doctores ecclesiae*)[53] have not been bishops of the Church.[54] In all ages theologians have been seen to be among the leading teachers in the Church, not least around the time of Vatican II. The importance of parents, teachers and priests must also not be underestimated. The teaching function of Christ is shared throughout the Church.[55]

Veritatis Splendor, however, insists that submitting to the *Magisterium* is not an abandonment of freedom, but the recognition of freedom within the truth. What the encyclical seems to fail to recognize is that moral laws cannot bring freedom whilst being externally imposed and not freely chosen, freely chosen because they are fully understood through carefully reasoned exposition of why they are good, leading to an acceptance and desire to do the good. This must, therefore, involve the conscience of every individual being respected, including those of theologians who are prepared to explore where the official teachers of the Church as yet may not wish to go.

Despite a claim within *Veritatis Splendor* that 'the Church's Magisterium does not intend to impose upon the faithful any particular theological system, still less a philosophical one' (VS, 29), this is difficult to verify. It certainly seems that there is an assumption that Roman Catholic ethics can be represented by the arguments of only one school of thought, namely that represented by Germain Grisez and John Finnis,[56] and one would certainly have great difficulty finding any commendation of any school, style, approach or method which falls outside that which is held by the Pope.[57] This is made all the more problematic and dangerous by the way in which 'dissent' and 'opposition' to the 'teaching of the Church's Pastors' (*VS* 113) are directly denounced.

The claims made in such ordinary teaching as that of *Veritatis Splendor* are, however, not absolute and are issued with assumptions of truth rather than guarantees of truth. Correct dissent is therefore possible and at times may indeed lead the Church to more appropriate teaching. As Lash asks, 'how else, from the dawning of the human mind, has truth been ascertained, mistakes corrected, confusion clarified, *except* through properly conducted disagreement?'[58] Such disagreement is clearly not encouraged by statements in *Veritatis Splendor* which view dissent as inadmissible and are also in danger of causing confusion, in the minds of many people, between the ordinary teaching of the Roman Catholic Church and the extension of its teaching authority to infallible statements, the latter requiring unconditional assent from church members. Infallible statements are, in fact, rare and there have been no such statements with respect to concrete moral questions.

The approach of *Veritatis Splendor* emphasizes the letter of the law and asserts the authority of the *'Magisterium'* and a submissive model of conscience, apparently claiming that personal conscience and reason cannot be set in opposition to the teaching of the *Magisterium*, and seemingly setting the authority of conscience and the Church in opposition. A similar line is taken in *The Catechism of the Catholic Church*.

The Catechism of the Catholic Church

Hughes[59] notes that the section on conscience in *The Catechism* combines the intensely personal tones of *Gaudium et Spes* with the reminder from the more technical definition of Alphonsus Liguori that conscience is not some kind of feeling but a judgement which is, therefore, accountable to reason. Johnstone, however, observes that it omits the following section of text from *GS* 16:

> In a marvellous manner conscience makes known that law which is fulfilled by the love of God and of neighbour. In their faithfulness to conscience, Christians are united with all other people in the search for truth and in finding true solutions to the many moral problems which arise in the lives of individuals in society.

This theme of love of God and neighbour is included in *Gaudium et Spes* in order to avoid a one-sided emphasis on natural law. Johnstone sees the omission of this passage from *The Catechism* as showing a preference for an interpretation which gives law priority over conscience, favouring a submissive model of conscience.[60]

The Catechism goes on to emphasise the importance of moral education and proper formation of conscience (1783–89). As Hughes notes, whilst there is much in the article which is straightforward and unexceptional there are two passages which, at the very least, could be seriously misleading.

> The education of conscience is indispensable for human beings who are subjected to negative influences and tempted by sin to prefer their own judgement and to reject authoritative teachings. (1783)

Ignorance of Christ and his Gospel, bad example given by others, enslavement to one's passions, assertion of a mistaken notion of autonomy of conscience, rejection of the Church's authority and her teaching, lack of conversion and of charity; these can be at the source of errors of judgement in moral conduct. (1792)

Whilst not asserting that a preference for one's own judgement amounts to being tempted by sin, the first passage, claims Hughes, could certainly easily be read that way. Such an interpretation would leave us with the ridiculous position of ruling out any dissent from one's parent, from the laws of the state and from non-infallible church teaching. Such a viewpoint, he suggests, is seriously misleading if only from the perspective that we have to judge the credentials of any given authority on a given point. Without denying the importance of educating one's conscience, Hughes believes that there should surely never be an abandonment of our own best judgement, in particular when judging whether or not the statements made by a given authority are acceptable. The second passage, Hughes feels, could equally be seen to be supporting the above interpretation of the first. Unfortunately, he says, there is no recognition in The *Catechism* that one might indeed be correct in dissenting from at least some non-infallible teaching.[61] As with *Veritatis Splendor*, a search for truth by the conscience, it seems to claim, can only result in submitting to the truth as interpreted by the *Magisterium*. There is a failure to acknowledge that there are examples where dissent from such teaching has been shown to be correct. Leo X, for example, condemned Martin Luther when the latter proposed that burning heretics at the stake was against God's Will. [62] Innocent IV allowed heretics to be tortured in order that they might[63] confess their wrongdoings and accuse others, despite this being condemned by Nicholas I in 866. This was also later condemned by Pius XII and is indeed condemned in *Veritatis Splendor* (*VS* 80). Other well known examples where dissent would have been correct concern slavery[64] and usury. The Catholic Church has also changed its teaching on religious liberty. As Preston notes, there is certainly no longer a call for 'all heathens, Jews and heretics and schismatics to go to hell unless converted to Catholicism'.[65] [66]

Whilst strongly emphasising the power of the *Magisterium*,

The Catechism (2038–39), in common with *Veritatis Splendor,* states that the Church needs 'the knowledge of theologians and the contribution of all men'. However, if it is to stand by this, the *Magisterium* must show that its teaching is based on revelation, reason and the experience of the whole Church. It can only achieve this through an obvious willingness seriously to consider the opinions and experiences of its members, a willingness which is not evident in its description of all dissent as unworthy of consideration. If its teaching is not grounded thus, then it is difficult to see how *The Catechism's* assertion that – 'Personal conscience and reason should not be set in opposition to the moral law or the Magisterium of the Church'[67] can be achieved.

Recent developments – theologians

Most theologians and psychologists today concentrate on addressing conscience as 'the reaction of our total personality to its proper functioning and disfunctioning, not to the functioning of this or that capacity but to the capacities which constitute our human and individual existence'.[68] Most accept conscience as more than just one faculty. It is no longer seen merely as a function of will or intellect, but ultimately as the whole person's commitment to values and the judgement that person makes in the light of that commitment to apply those values. Such an holistic view of conscience allows us to appreciate the three dimensions of conscience subscribed to in more recent developments among moral theologians within the Roman Catholic tradition, three dimensions which are not different realities or stages of conscience, but three different ways of understanding conscience.

Conscience/1 (*Synderesis*) is seen as a given characteristic of being human which provides us with the capacity for knowing and doing good and avoiding evil. It provides us with the shared general sense of moral good, and the general sense that doing what is good and avoiding evil makes a difference. The great array of moral disagreements experienced in everyday life confirm rather than negate the existence of conscience/1. The existence of this orientation to the good makes the lively debate over what is right and what is wrong, in each case of moral choice, possible. We cannot live morally without conscience/1, but alone it is not enough to enable us to choose what is right in each specific situation.

Conscience/1, it is claimed, empowers us to *seek* the objective moral values in each situation in order to do what is right. It is conscience/2, however, that does the work of *discovering* the operative moral values and the right thing to do. Its primary tasks are accurate perception and right moral reasoning. Conscience/2 has received much attention in moral debate and education, because it is seen as the realm of moral blindness and insight, moral disagreement and error. It is conscience/2 which is subject to the process of the 'formation of conscience' and needs to be educated, informed, examined and transformed. The aim of this process is 'correct seeing and right thinking', which is achieved by the formation of conscience/2 in community, and by using a wide range of sources of moral wisdom.

Conscience/3 moves us from perception and reasoning to action. The general orientation to the good (conscience/1) and the process of considering the relevant moral factors (conscience/2) converge to produce conscience/3, the judgement of what the person must do in a particular situation and the commitment to do it. The judgement of conscience/3 is always a judgement for ME. It is not a judgement of what someone else can do, it can only be a judgement of what I can do. The essential part of the dignity and freedom of conscience is present in conscience/3 – I must always do what I believe to be right and avoid what I believe to be wrong. If an individual believes in his or her heart, that is, with his or her whole person, that a specific course of action is God's objective call, that course of action becomes essential. It becomes a moral requirement for that person, as identified in Vatican II.[69]

> In asking "What ought I to do?" one poses a question about "moral knowledge" contained in conscience and about the content which will be given as an answer. Each person must find this answer for himself: once it is found, however, precisely because it is given by conscience, this answer reveals itself as an absolute demand which concerns the total person endowed with freedom – his entire destiny and salvation.[70]

In the final analysis, it is said, conscience can be the only sure guide for action by a free and knowing person. To violate conscience/3 is to violate one's personal integrity. There is a danger, however, of individualism and of isolating conscience from other sources of moral wisdom. Conscience/2 must carry on the dialogue with sources of moral knowledge in order to ensure the trustworthiness of conscience/3, which can only be proportionate to the work which is carried out in forming one's conscience.[71]

A healthy conscience occurs where the whole person functions in harmony, which includes the emotional, the intellectual and the energies of will.[72] It is also recognized, however, that a person's intellect and will are somehow distinct and can oppose each other, creating a painful rift. The intellect's longing for truth is shaken when, out of sinister motives, the will opposes it. The will also agonizes as it tries to withstand the intellect's longing for improved knowledge and realization of the good.

For Häring this longing for integration can only be complete when one accepts the longing of the intellect and will to be united in truth, and accepts that this integration draws us to God and to others. He sees self-understanding and the furthering of the individual's knowledge of good to be dependent upon the symbols created by the interaction of many minds in mutual human relationship. Responding to the longing for dignity and wholeness in others gives us a greater knowledge of self. This relates to the covenant dimension of conscience found in Jeremiah (Jer 31.31–33). God speaks of making a new covenant with his people and of writing his law upon their hearts, this law being 'Love your neighbour as yourself' (Matt. 7.12, Luke 6.31). The mature Christian conscience understands the inner law through Christ's example of the covenant, 'Love one another as I have loved you' (John 15.12) . [73]

Reciprocity of conscience

The mutuality of conscience is indicated in its Latin root, *con (cum)* and *scientia,* which means 'knowing together'. According to the Roman Catholic tradition, wholesome rela-

tionships, based on mutual love and respect, are very important in the development of a mature and healthy conscience,
the reciprocal arrangement being that a healthy and mature
conscience, in its turn, allows the development of wholesome
relationships between individuals and within the community.
This does not deny that self-reflection and self-awareness are
essential to conscience, but these cannot genuinely develop
without the experience of relationships with others. Genuine
reciprocity of conscience requires a meeting between individuals, in which their individuality and personal identity are
respected. It requires an acceptance of each other's differences
and equal dignity which leads to a real respect for each other's
conscience, and, as a result, a freeing from the superego
(which we shall discuss later), a freedom from playing roles
to please each other. This allows each person to be their own
person, whilst providing a place of unity where individuals
can be a source of identity, integrity and authenticity for each
other.

An individualistic perspective on conscience does not seem
to be the approach taken in Scripture. Indeed in Romans 14
and 1 Corinthians 10 we find Paul's discussion of a specific
example of reciprocity of conscience. He addresses the issue
of care required by those who have developed in faith for
those who have weaker consciences and notes the need to
respect the consciences of everyone.

> For instance, one person will have the faith to eat all kinds of
> food, while a weaker one eats only vegetables. The person who
> eats must not hold in contempt the other who does not, and he
> who does not eat must not pass judgement on the one who does;
> for God has accepted him. (Rom. 14.2–3)[74]

Genuine reciprocity of conscience, however, needs to be
distinguished from a superficial reciprocity of conscience.
Superficial reciprocity consists in members of a group
convincing each other that their actions are right whilst these
actions are merely based on mimicry of the powerful, there
being a lack of discernment on the part of the individuals. The
spirit and the system of apartheid in South Africa is used by
Häring[75] as a prime example of such destructive reciprocity of
conscience. Within this system the powerful and ruling white

class constantly confirmed its members' belief that, because they were white and successful, they were superior. The acceptance of such a system as unchangeable by some of the black population meant that they too were imprisoned by this superficial form of reciprocity of conscience, in that they accepted the system and even looked up to the powerful whites. Such a reciprocity of conscience only unites the group whilst it upholds their selfish goals. It leads to division, however, when a disadvantaged individual or part of the group wants what the others have. The only way forward from this impasse is genuine dialogue which respects the consciences of others and considers the experience and reflection of all.

The Church itself, whilst providing examples of genuine reciprocity of conscience, is not immune to superficial reciprocity of conscience based upon group cohesion and a process of reinforcement. Such groups can often be seen to develop their own survival system, grounded in suspicion of outsiders who think and act differently. Whilst such a system may provide group cohesion, it is dangerous in that it can eventually prevent its members from respecting the dignity of conscience of others and even the dignity of their own individual consciences.

Reciprocity of conscience and natural law

In Romans, Paul comments upon the relationship between Jewish and Gentile Christians and calls for mutual respect. In Roman Catholic writings, this is often seen in the context of natural law.[76]

> God has no favourites ... When Gentiles who do not have the Law carry out precepts by the light of nature, then, although they are their own law, they display the substance of the law inscribed on their hearts. Their conscience is called as witness, and their own thoughts argue the case on either side, against them or for them, on the day when God judges the secrets of the human heart through Christ Jesus (Rom. 2.11–16)

Paul sees the Law as the love of God and of neighbour. Individuals, therefore, learn to discern what complies with the law written on their 'hearts' not just through intellectual dialogue but through learning from the demands of love made through relationships which involve shared experience and reflection. *Gaudium et Spes* para 16, in its discourse on conscience, makes direct reference to Rom. 2.15 and follows this with a discussion of the reciprocity of conscience with respect to both Christians and non-Christians.[77] 'In fidelity to conscience, Christians are joined with the rest of men in the search for truth, and for the genuine solution to the numerous problems which arise in the life of individuals and from social relationships.'[78] Interestingly, this section is omitted from The *Catechism*, as indicated earlier in this chapter.

Love of neighbour, and therefore dialogue with others, is part of the very nature of the individual. Self-identity is achieved through openness to God and to others, and it is within conscience that one comes to the fullness of openness to others. Hence, according to much Roman Catholic literature, natural law arises through shared experience and reflection. The genuine search for truth and faithfulness to conscience cannot, therefore, occur without the individual being open to others.

Such a standpoint on reciprocity of conscience means that natural law, that which is written on the 'heart', is not a code but arises from the dynamics of love relationships with others and with God. Remote applications of natural law cannot therefore be time bound. Humanity can look to past experience, but it is also constantly faced with new dilemmas which further increase as the dialogue between different groups and cultures increases. This means that the Roman Catholic Church has a responsibility to enter into and learn from worldwide dialogue if it is to hold authority as an effective teacher with respect to natural law.[79]

Reciprocity of conscience and church authority

Häring emphasizes the supreme authority under God of the sincere conscience and the importance of reciprocity of conscience in order to achieve a mature conscience. This clearly leaves us with the question of the role of the authority of the church. Häring points out the important educational and strengthening role played, with respect to conscience, by the authority of conscientious persons who are competent in important areas of life. He goes on to highlight the increased 'authority' enjoyed by the office-holders of the church when they are fully appreciative of the 'prophets and many humble saints who live fully the reciprocity of consciences under God and in full co-responsibility with and for all God's people'. The authority and flourishing of the church, and in particular the *Magisterium*, is promoted when they become outstanding listeners and observers. Those who are charged as guardians and promoters of the faith 'can be leaders of the people only if they are the most outstanding listeners, listening to the word of God, listening to each other, listening to the faithful, especially to those who embody the moral and religious authority of life, competence and experience, while listening always to the Spirit who prompts their hearts to search, in absolute sincerity, for truth'.[80]

For Häring, given the current difficulties of changing and transitory times, and the effects of globalization, it is of paramount importance that this involves the *Magisterium* co-operating with theologians to achieve a greater understanding of issues of the time. Theologians also, however, need to respect the teaching of those in authority and to be aware that their consciences should also be attentive to the needs of the time. They must nevertheless pass on to the *Magisterium* what is perceived by their own consciences. There needs to be an environment which fosters respect and co-operation, where conscience can speak to conscience.[81]

There is no desire on Häring's part to deny the authority of those who teach and make decisions, and indeed he acknowledges the need for loyalty and obedience towards them. The quality of this authority and obedience, however, needs to be understood in relation to the common faith of all Christians, to be shared and more effectively understood through the reciprocity of consciences. It is when the importance and place of reciprocity of consciences is acknowledged and respected that Magisterial interventions and the research of theologians will strengthen the teaching authority of the Church. The development and maturity of conscience is more effectively promoted through the example of those living truthfully under the authority of their individual conscience, whilst wholly respecting the consciences of others, than by submission to abstract laws. Its faithfulness to Christ and the authenticity of the *Magisterium* will be achieved by its primary aim being honesty, sincerity and responsibility rather than through an emphasis on submission which relies on superego morality.[82]

Recent developments – psychology

Superego and the development of conscience

It is clear that within social processes and relationships, and within the psyche, there are factors which restrict our freedom to choose and to act. One such factor, which must be taken into account in any serious attempt to grapple with the Roman Catholic notion of conscience, is the agency Freud called the superego. We must differentiate between 'superego' and conscience in order to understand the goals of committing rather than submitting one's freedom, and those of developing one's character.

What is generally considered to be normal development moves from a conscience controlled externally – one which is based upon obeying someone in authority or doing as others do – to one which is much more internally directed: one based on our acting in a way that we as individuals see as right. Therefore, to mature, individuals must become their own persons and make decisions for themselves. Someone who spends the whole of life submitting to authority, spends it submitting their freedom rather than committing it. A morally mature person is, therefore, one who can perceive, choose and identify with the actions they undertake. Each choice taken is, hence, a choice between being an authentic or an inauthentic person, a choice to act either in or out of character.

The 'superego' can be seen as 'the ego of another superimposed on our own to serve as an internal censor to regulate our conduct using guilt as its powerful weapon'.[83] It develops through the basic childhood instinct for self-preservation, a drive to maintain the love and approval of the adults upon whom the child is dependent. Children develop and identify the types of behaviour which evoke positive and negative responses, and in order to prevent disapproval and withdrawal of love, they embrace the standards of those in authority. The superego stores all their 'should's' and 'have to's'. As identified by Callaghan, 'the instructions/demands of the superego arise not from reflection, but from past "recordings" described as the "unconscious internalisation of what were experienced as the expectations and demands of those whose approval was vital to the developing individual".'[84] Most of these 'internalizations' occur below the level of consciousness. It is not that children are reflectively aware that to do this or that displeases, but that they 'feel bad' at the thought of doing this or that. This feeling comes to be characterized as guilt, or, to be more exact, guilt in one of its forms – superego guilt.

Conscience differs from the superego. Instead of being concerned with the 'shoulds' and 'have tos' of someone else, it is concerned with the personal decisions of the individual. It acts through love responding to the call to commit oneself to value, as opposed to the superego which responds to the need for acceptance, love and approval. The moral conscience looks to personalized, internalized values, whereas the superego looks to authority. For the Christian the confusion of conscience and superego is seen in the attempt to differentiate between God's calling enabling them to act and what someone in authority tells them to do. This tension was highlighted above when we considered the official teaching of the Roman Catholic Church with respect to authority and the sovereignty of conscience.

Erikson, Fromm and many others were particularly concerned with ensuring that the superego was assigned its proper role. It does have its function within specific limits, but its legitimate function is at the more primitive levels of the psyche. In childhood and early adolescence the superego plays an important part in progress towards a mature conscience. It can be an important aid to socialization. In adults, when integrated into a mature conscience, it can relieve us from the need to decide afresh every time a matter arises which has already been legitimately determined by convention and custom. If at the right time individuals work out for themselves that they are in agreement with the basic orientation towards the good found within the superego, the energies of the superego can be channelled along the same path. This results in a mature peaceful conscience, an integration of person and the integrity of covenant morality, covenant morality opening the individual to a new and creative response to God and others. If, however, the superego is distorted through a system of education which enforces obedience, it can draw an individual into collective sinfulness and, at best, a superego morality which tends to be sterile, repetitive and degrading. Erikson and Fromm, amongst others, warned against a false education which builds only the superego. The superego gains overpowering strength through the emotions caused by fear of authority and by an education based on the pain-and-pleasure principles, whilst the conscience, as such, is overlooked. Educators and moralists who rely upon conventional morals concerned with external rules and those whose trust is placed mainly in sanctions and rewards are strong allies to the superego.

This means that there is a need to respect the difference between the superego and the conscience in 'pastoral counselling'. In serving the superego one would concentrate on an individual's actions divorced from their overall context. An approach addressing the development of a mature moral conscience, however, would address the overall context of a person's life and the values deserving preference, given the context. One of the tasks of moral education is to reduce the influence of the superego and allow a genuinely personal way of seeing and responding to be established. Education based on the gospel should not reinforce the superego but gradually free one from it.

> The person who is dominated by the superego has the accuser, judge and tormentor all wrapped up in one, built into his own psychic make-up. When such a person hears the Christian message given with an accent on God as judge, he can project his superego on this divinity and use religion as an instrument to subject himself to this court and, unknown to himself, to promote his own unconscious self-hatred.[85]

Superego and problems for maturity

Brendan Callaghan[86] holds that, whilst providing us with the most human (and therefore incarnately divine) way of dealing with the experience of guilt, the Christian tradition has also warped our understanding of sin and guilt. He refers in particular to the overall image of God which traditions give Christians. Rowan Williams wrote of Martin Luther :

> Luther, looked, with rare simplicity, into the face of the God he was told to serve and *hated* what he saw. God was a righteous God – that was taken for granted – and he demanded conformity to his righteousness and condemned failure to conform. He demanded whole-heartedness, but how could the endlessly self-regarding, self-observing, self-dividing human soul produce such simplicity? Nothing in human motivation could be clear; by what right can a person ever satisfy himself or herself that an action is 'good'? By no right; Luther found this out through years of self-torture in the confessional.[87]

The image of a demanding God which Luther saw and hated is not uncommon, an image which for Callaghan is portrayed in Gerard Hughes' book *God of Surprises*. For Callaghan, holding on to such an image leaves us with a diminished image in the place of a living God, and produces difficulties in dealing with sin and guilt. If our primary perception of God is as a judge to be feared, there will be a strong temptation to hold on to the superego. There is a vast difference between this and seeing God as a God of love providing the support and strength required to take what may be perceived as the risk of developing a mature conscience.

Ultimately, nevertheless, the experience and reality of sin must be faced. Ultimately, I am the only one who can take responsibility and, within this, I have to acknowledge that I can never be certain that the decision I make is the right one, but I must make it anyway. Taking this risk, however, involves giving up childhood omnipotence, whilst at the same time acting as though our decisions are right. From one theological perspective at least, normal guilt therefore requires that we drop any attempt at perfection, that is, any attempt to be God. Normal guilt means we must accept the limitations of being human. Repressing and denying the reality of the human situation leads to neurotic guilt.

Relinquishing the superego, and its control of the individual's behaviour so as to meet the expectations of others, also means relinquishing perfection, which is painful. It means recognizing personal limits, whilst at the same time recognizing that the dependence on others that you have sought is neither possible nor necessary. This results in a deep sense of loss and mourning for this strange mixture of total dependence and total omnipotence. Dependence on superego works from the basis that I can be totally dependent on you if, and only if, I am totally capable of being who you want me to be. Dependence and omnipotence go hand in hand. If dependence on superego is not relinquished, however, we are left with nothing more than meeting the expectations of others.

Callaghan notes, that, paradoxically, this relinquishing of the omnipotent fantasies of infancy is the start of that genuine love of self that the gospel calls us to.[88] Pierre Solignac expressed it as follows :

> Love of self calls for a great deal of lucidity, objectivity and courage. To accept oneself is to accept communicating with oneself and to appreciate one's qualities and failings, one's potentialities and limitations. It is to succeed in living without being perpetually relative to someone else or to some rule or other which has been more or less well internalised. Finally, it is to accept being fully responsible for oneself, one's life and one's choices.[89]

It is our inability to take responsibility for ourselves, our lives, and our choices, says Callaghan, that drives us to try to live as omnipotent, omniscient and all-loving and to rely on the superego. Taking responsibility may at first sight be asserting an autonomy which appears to challenge God's sovereignty, but it instead turns out to be an expression of an individual's relationship to that sovereignty. Vatican II, indeed, states:

> Authentic freedom is an exceptional sign of the divine image within man. For God has willed that man be left 'in the hand of his own counsel' (Sir. 15:4) so that he can seek his Creator spontaneously, and come freely to utter and blissful perfection through loyalty to Him. Hence man's dignity demands that he act according to a knowing and free choice. Such a choice is personally motivated and prompted from within. It does not result from blind internal impulse nor from mere external pressure.[90]

Taking responsibility, nevertheless, appears to be something we find difficult almost to the point of impossibility, because it removes us from that infantile state of 'omnipotent dependence'.[91]

Callaghan goes on to say that it would be good if the life and teaching of the Roman Catholic Church had encouraged this move towards genuine self-love, the development of a mature conscience and taking responsibility for ourselves. He does not, however, see how this could be honestly stated to be the case. The Roman Catholic Church, he claims, has often fostered immaturity and boosted superego mechanisms at the expense of conscience[92]. Indeed the emphasis on written law and obedience to the *Magisterium* and its interpretation of that law, found in recent Roman Catholic documents could be cited as an example of this very approach, an approach which has been criticised for possibly leading to complacency.

The Roman Catholic Church cannot make individuals' moral decisions for them, but can only provide them with guidance. This church, even post-Vatican II, has, nevertheless, continued to take definitive stands on certain issues, for example, abortion, contraception and pre-marital sex. It is important to recognize that, whilst the church may hold such a position, effective teaching in such areas is achieved by concentrating not upon the rule itself but upon the reason for holding it. Without attention to and effective discussion of such reasons the *Magisterium* cannot expect effectively to perform its role as the official teaching authority of the Roman Catholic church and assist the development of mature consciences within its community.[93]

There is a need for the developing individual, through moral education, to be assisted in progressing towards higher levels of moral development. This means moral education assisting in appreciation of the difference between ethical principles and arbitrary rules, beliefs, customs or traditions. It also requires that those in authority operate on a basis of the sharing of knowledge as opposed to one of control and submission, encouraging and providing individuals with the ability to become involved in moral judgement and discourse for themselves as opposed to those in authority imposing a specific morality.

If persons are to be fully mature, it is necessary that they become their own persons following their own principles of judgement and action. This means accepting a group, which includes the community of the church, because, independently of any authority and being true to their own conscience, they can live with that group. No group mind should be allowed to replace the conscience of the individual. It should surely only be involved in assisting with the education and formation of conscience/2.

Conclusion

In discussing what is meant by a mature Christian conscience within the Roman Catholic tradition we face the tension for that Church between freedom of conscience and authority, and between a concern for the spirit of the law with an emphasis on the development of the mature person and the idea of freedom, and concern for the letter of the law, the role of the *Magisterium* as moral guardian and its concern that the law is disseminated and adhered to. This in turn provides a tension within the sphere of moral education, the *Magisterium* on the one hand adopting the role of teaching correct moral precepts and on the other being concerned with developing virtuous and mature individuals, and respecting the dignity of individual consciences. The former pays little attention to the reason for laws, moral maturity being judged simply by adherence to such laws, whilst the latter is concerned with free and sponta- neous acceptance of God's will, not blind acceptance through superego morality. If, however, the aim is to allow mature moral development it would seem from the above discussion that this is achieved, at least partially, through an emphasis on improving the individual's level of reasoning on certain issues through effective education of conscience/2.

Encouraging mature moral development means the Church encouraging individuals to be more self sufficient and not excessively dependent upon it, this necessarily involving the risk that such adults who freely choose the Church are equally free to choose not to be a part of it. Individuals returning to the Church, however, will do so in greater maturity having accepted for themselves the values and practices it claims. Duska and Whelan[94] are of the opinion that this was the very risk that the Roman Catholic Church appeared to be prepared to take in Vatican II. Before that Council, the 'good' Roman Catholic could have been viewed as existing within a religious enclave where individuals believed and passionately defended the system and its absolutes and fixed rules. Relaxing restrictions against mixed marriages, allowing individuals to join groups like the YMCA and gradually discarding the index of forbidden books allowed Roman Catholics increasingly to see their church alongside other groups and in particular other churches. This clearly can be and was a painful process for many, as it means moving on from the certainty of rules and regulations towards an increasing dependence on the dignity and integrity of one's own conscience and away from any superego morality, remembering always that, as Häring notes, this does not mean that a good conscience is a matter of self-assurance and self-affirmation. Believers stand before God, who is their divine Judge and Saviour (1 Cor. 4.4), and do not make a judgement of conscience individualistically, being ever concerned for the integrity of the conscience of others (1 Cor. 10. 25–29).

Being asked to look upon an institution previously regarded as divine and free from error as one which is human and which has the usual human flaws, difficulties and limitations can cause a major crisis. It is at this point that there is a great need for Christian moral educators who can replace the promulgation of absolute laws and conditioned acceptance of a system with understanding, guidance and encouragement for the person who is striving towards greater maturity and free commitment towards the Church and its primary aims, alongside a recognition of its limitations. Whilst this appeared to be the approach of Vatican II, it is difficult to verify the continuation of this approach in the more recent Vatican documents, *Veritatis Splendor* and *The Catechism of the Catholic Church*. There, indeed, appears to be some backtracking from the approach of Vatican II, the current emphasis being on obedience to the teaching of the *Magisterium* (all dissent being inadmissible) and a submissive model of conscience.

Notes

1   Unless stated otherwise, the term 'Magisterium' is used throughout this study in the narrow sense of meaning the official teaching authority of the Catholic Church as represented by the pope and the bishops.

2   R. Schnackenburg, *Moral Teaching of the New Testament* (New York), 1965, pp 69f, as cited in Bernard Häring, *Free and Faithful in Christ*, vol.1, (Paulist Press, New York, 1989), p. 225.

3   Bernard Häring, *Free and Faithful in Christ*, vol. 1, pp. 226–227.

4   Wendell Lee Willis, *Idol Meat in Corinth: The Pauline Argument in 1 Corinthians 8 and 10* (Scholars Press, Chico, California, 1985), p. 89.

5   For further details see chapter 1 above, Helen Costigane, 'A History of the Western Idea of Conscience'.

6   Phillipe Delhaye, *The Christian Conscience* (New York, 1968), p. 36.

7   Willis, op. cit., p. 91.

8   T. J. Deidun, *New Covenant Morality in Paul* (Biblical Institute Press, Rome, 1981), p. 161.

9   Victor Paul Furnish, *Theology and Ethics in Paul* (Abingdon Press, New York, 1968), p. 48, p. 229.

10 John Mahoney, *The Making of Moral Theology* (Clarendon Press, Oxford, 1987), p. 185.

11 Furnish, op cit., p. 229.

12 As cited in Willis, op. cit., p. 91.

13 Delhaye, op. cit., pp. 48–49.

14 Mahoney, op. cit., p. 186.

15 Häring, *Free and Faithful...*, p. 229.

16 Deidun, op. cit., p. 161.

17 J. Paul Sampley, *Walking between the Times: Paul's Moral Reasoning* (Fortress Press, Minneapolis, 1991), p. 58.

18 Furnish, op. cit., p. 229.

19 Willis, op. cit., p. 92.

20 R. E. O. White, *Biblical Ethics: The Changing Continuity of Biblical Ethics,* vol. 1. (Paternoster Press, Exeter, 1979), p. 141.

21 W. Lillie, *Studies in New Testament Ethics*, (Oliver & Boyd, Edinburgh, 1961), pp. 45f, 54 as cited in White, op. cit., p. 139.

22 H. W. Robinson, *Christian Doctrine of Man* (T & T Clark, Edinburgh (3rd edition), 1926), p. 107, as cited in White, op. cit., p. 139.

23 The word 'conscience 'is derived from the Latin, *cum* (together) and *scientia, scire* (to know).

24 The word *synteresis* is thought by most theologians to have probably appeared in theological reflection through a corruption of *syneidesis* in the commentary of St Jerome on Ezekiel. Mahoney, however, challenges this common assumption. See John Mahoney, op cit., p. 187.

25 Paul Lehmann, 'The Decline and Fall of Conscience', in C. Ellis Nelson, *Conscience: theological and psychological perspectives* (Newman Press, New York, 1973), p. 31.

26 Häring, *Free and Faithful...*, p. 230.

27 Mahoney, *op. cit.*, pp. 187–188.

28 *De Veritate*, q.16, art.1; q.17, art.1. Quoted from the English translation entitled *Truth*, by James V. McGlynn (Henry Reguery Company), 1953, and cited in Lehmann, op. cit., p. 31.

29 Häring, *Free and Faithful...*, pp. 230–231.

30 ibid., pp. 231–32.

31 Delhaye, op. cit, p. 111.

32 Häring, *Free and Faithful...*, pp. 231–232.

33 More detailed analysis of Scripture and early writers can be found in chapter 1 above, Helen Costigane, 'A History of the Western Idea of Conscience'.

34 For further details on the roots of natural law see Richard M. Gula, *Reason Informed by Faith* (Paulist Press, New York, 1989), pp. 221–223.

35 Gula, op. cit., p. 224.

36 Paul in Rom. 2.14–16 is often seen as referring to natural law when he claims that the gentiles have a law within themselves which is God given. It is referred to as a law written in their 'hearts' and is often aligned to conscience. There have, however, been objections to these claims and other claims of reference to natural law in the New Testament. For further discussion see Bruno Schüller, 'A Contribution to the Theological Discussion of Natural Law' in Charles E. Curran and Richard A. McCormick (eds), *Readings in Moral Theology No.7: Natural Law and Theology* (Paulist Press, New York, 1991), pp. 72–98.

37 Gula, op. cit., pp. 224–225.

38 Retention of Ulpian's definition can be found in *Summa Theologiae*, 1-2, q.94, art.2.

39 This stems from Aristotle's ontology and teleology, that is, something is good if it lives up to its purpose; human beings are good when they fulfil the purpose of being human. Moral goodness is acting as a fulfilled human being.

40   Again Aquinas is seen here to pick up on the teaching of Aristotle, in that Aristotle saw humans to be basically social animals.

41   For further information, see Charles E. Curran, 'Natural Law and Moral Theology', in Charles E. Curran and Richard A. McCormick, *Readings in Moral Theology No.7: Natural Law and Theology,* pp. 247–295.

42   *See Gula,* op. cit., p. 234.

43   As cited in Gula, op. cit., p. 238.

44   The traditional couplet of 'faith and morals' is found first in a major statement of one of the early decrees of the Council of Trent. The translation, however, of the Latin word '*mores*' into 'morals' is in doubt, as in its singular form '*mos*' it is used to mean an 'established practice or custom, or usage', without any particular reference to morality. It may be more appropriate to use the couplet 'faith and religious practices' in some contexts of Trent. For further information see John Mahoney, op cit., chapter 4.

45   The Pastoral Constitution on the Church in the Modern World, *Gaudium et Spes,* para. 16, in Austin Flannery (ed.), *Vatican Council II: The Conciliar and Post Conciliar Documents,* (Gracewing Fowler Wright, Leominster, 1981).

46   Declaration on Religious Liberty, *Dignitatis humanae,* para 3, in Flannery, op. cit.

47   Nicholas Lash, 'Crisis and Tradition in *Veritatis Splendor*', *Studies in Christian Ethics,* vol.7, no.2, 1994, p. 23

48   Lash, op. cit., p. 23

49   Nicholas Peter Harvey, 'Comment on *Veritatis Splendor*', *Studies in Christian Ethics,* vol.7, no.2, 1994, p. 14

50   Harvey, op. cit., pp. 14–15.

51   Within this context David Brown explains 'intellectual' as 'ensuring that one's judgements are based on what the facts really are', and 'imaginative' as 'ensuring one's sympathies properly extend beyond just the confines of those most like oneself'. See David Brown, 'The Role of Conscience' in Charles Yeats (ed.), *Veritatis Splendor – A Response* (The Canterbury Press, Norwich, 1994), pp. 32–33.

52   Ronald Preston, '*Veritatis Splendor:* A Comment', *Studies in Christian Ethics,* vol. 7, no. 2, 1994, p. 40.

53   The Roman Catholic Church names as *doctores* individuals who have taught the Church. It is not an office but a post-factum recognition of a service. See John Coventry, *Christian Truth,* (Darton, Longman & Todd, London, 1975), p.77.

54 These include lay members like Teresa of Avila, priests like Jerome and John of the Cross and, of course, the theologian and priest Thomas Aquinas. Others like Augustine and John Chrysostom were made bishops because of their abilities as great teachers, not the other way around.

55 John Coventry, *Christian Truth,* pp. 76–78.

56 For further details see Germain Grisez, *The Way of the Lord Jesus: vol. 1, Christian Moral Principles* (Franciscan Herald Press, Chicago, 1983), and Germain Grisez, John Finnis and Joseph Boyle, 'Practical Principles, Moral Truth and Ultimate Ends', *The American Journal of Jurisprudence,* vol. 32, 1987.

57 Lash, op. cit., p. 25.

58 ibid., p. 26.

59 Gerard J. Hughes, 'Our Human Vocation' in Michael J. Walsh (ed.), *Commentary on the Catechism of the Catholic Church* (Geoffrey Chapman, London, 1994), p. 348.

60 Brian V. Johnstone, 'Erroneous Conscience in Veritatis Splendor and the Theological Tradition', in Joe Selling and Jan Jans (eds), *The Splendor of Accuracy: An Examination of the Assertion made by Veritatis Splendor* (Kok Pharos Publishing, The Netherlands, 1994), pp. 116–117.

61 Hughes, op. cit., p. 349.

62 Bernard Hoose, *Received Wisdom?: Reviewing the Role of Tradition in Christian Ethics* (Geoffrey Chapman, London, 1994), p. 20.

63 See Hoose, op. cit., p. 4, for further details.

64 See Hoose, op. cit., p.63, and John F. Maxwell, *Slavery and the Catholic Church,* (Barry Rose Publishers, London, 1975), for further details.

65 Ronald Preston, op cit., p. 40.

66 See Hoose, op. cit., pp. 160–1 for further details.

67 Hughes, op. cit., p. 350.

68 Fromm, *Man for Himself* (Greenwich, 1969), p. 149, as cited in Häring, *Free and Faithful...,* p. 296.

69 Gula, *Reason Informed by Faith,* pp. 130–134.

70 Josef Fuchs, *Personal Responsibility and Christian Morality,* p. 219.

71 Gula, *Reason Informed by Faith,* pp. 130–134.

72 This can be related back to Augustine and the Trinitarian view of the person – wholeness occurring when these three are in harmony.

73 Häring, *Free and Faithful...,* pp. 236–237.

74 Additional examples of references by Paul to reciprocity of

conscience can also be found in Bernard Häring, 'Conscience: The Sanctuary of Creative Fidelity and Liberty', in R. P. Hamel and K. R. Himes (eds), *Introduction to Christian Ethics,* pp. 274–276.

75 Bernard Häring, 'Reciprocity of Consciences: A Key Concept in Moral Theology', in R. Gallagher and B. McConvery (eds), *History and Conscience* (Gill & Macmillan, Dublin, 1989), p. 62.

76 See endnote 36.

77 One of the primary assets of natural law is that the Roman Catholic Church can claim to teach both Christians and non-Christians, both being able to discern the truth through natural law.

78 Vatican II, The Pastoral Constitution on the Church in the Modern World, *Gaudium et Spes,* para 16.

79 Häring, 'Reciprocity of Consciences..', pp. 65–68.

80 Archbishop Robert Coffi, *Lehramt und Theologie – Die Situation heute,* in *Orientierung* 40 (1976), 63–66, as cited in Häring, 'Conscience : The Sanctuary...', p. 276.

81 Häring, 'Reciprocity of Consciences...', p. 68.

82 Häring, 'Conscience: The Sanctuary....', pp. 273–277.

83 Richard Gula, *Reason Informed by Faith,* p. 124

84 Brendan Callaghan, "The tragic experience of consciousness': psychological reflections on sin and guilt', *The Month,* Sept/Oct 1993, p. 397.

85 G. Baum, *Man Becoming* (New York), 1971, p. 223, cited in Bernard Häring, *Free and Faithful in Christ:* Vol. 1, p. 234.

86 Callaghan, op. cit., p. 397.

87 Rowan Williams, *The Wound of Knowledge,* pp. 143–144, as cited in Callaghan, op. cit., p. 398.

88 One assumes from this that Callaghan is referring to Matt 22.19 – 'Love your neighbour *as yourself'.* See also Lev. 19.18, Rom. 13.9 and Gal. 5.14.

89 Pierre Solignac, *The Christian Neurosis,* p. 127, as cited in Callaghan, op. cit., p. 400.

90 Walter M. Abbott, (ed), *The Documents of Vatican II,* America Press, 1966, p. 214, as cited in Ronald Duska and Mariellen Whelan, *Moral Development: A Guide to Piaget and Kohlberg,* (Gill & Macmillan, Dublin, 1977), pp. 90–91.

91 Callaghan, op. cit., p. 400.

92 ibid.

93 Duska and Whelan, op. cit., ch. III.

94 Duska and Whelan, op. cit., p. 95.

4

Conscience in Orthodox Thought

Stephen Thomas

Introduction: conscience in ancient thought

Eastern and western Christians alike have acquired from Stoicism a grand idea, that of natural law, which has had a profound effect on civic and personal morality and on religion. This idea is that nature is the guide for human behaviour and that reason brings knowledge of an inward law. This innate moral knowledge came to be known as conscience (*conscientia*) through Marcus Tullius Cicero, the great orator, republican and eclectic popularizer of Greek philosophy. More a Stoic than anything else, in his last years before his judicial murder as the Republic collapsed before the totalitarianism of the first triumvirate, he formulated the famous dictum that the 'true law' is 'right reason in agreement with nature ... of universal application, unchanging and everlasting'. He declared that the knowledge of right and wrong was to be found in the human consciousness: 'We need not look outside ourselves for an interpreter of it'.[1]

This innate inward interpreter Cicero called *conscientia*, a 'knowing with', that is, a moral awareness or capacity for judgment, a knowing in company with oneself. It is also a 'knowing with' others, for the validity of the inward insight is confirmed by the agreement of others, both being in harmony with nature.   The exact Greek etymological equivalent of *conscientia* in Greek is *syneidesis* and this is the term used in the Greek Bible and in Byzantine theology and political philosophy.

The Christian Roman Empire, from the fourth century onwards based in Byzantium, the New Rome, inherited the Stoic tradition. The Emperor Justinian who controlled the East and who still exerted considerable power over the collapsing West, initiated the compilation of the *Corpus Juris Civilis* in AD 534 . It is a collection of writings on law going back to the old Roman Empire, before its political breakup under barbarian incursions, and an attempt to recivilize the Italy which he was trying to reconquer. The guiding idea of this collection, which has so influenced western philosophy of law is epitomized in the statements of Gaius, a classical lawyer, whose work, dating *c.*AD 160, is quoted in the *Digest*, that part of the *Corpus Juris Civilis* which collected excerpts from earlier jurists: 'What natural reason dictates to all men and is most equally observed among them is called the law of nations, as that law which is practised by all mankind'.[2]

Another early jurist, quoted in the *Digest*, Ulpian (third century AD), speaks of a 'natural instinct' which all animals have and declares the 'natural instinct' proper to the human animal to be about 'the law of nations'.[3] The antithesis, therefore, between western legal practicality, and Eastern theocracy cannot be strictly maintained. Eastern and western Christians alike share the inheritance of an immutable natural law which human beings can discern by virtue of natural instinct, natural reason, or conscience, the innate capacity to judge right and wrong. It is, however, debatable whether or not Justinian was typical of eastern Christian attitudes in his approach to natural law. Justinian was a politician. In Eastern Orthodoxy *syneidesis* never attained the sense of an autonomous, innate, faculty of judgement, as it often has in Western theological thought.

The Stoic tradition of natural law, moreover, asserted that nature was guided by the divine *Logos*, the *anima mundi,* so that there was a providence (*pronoia*) upon which human kind could depend.[4] In Cleanthes' famous hymn to Zeus, the god has become the one God, 'O God most glorious, called by many a name'. Knowledge of God and obedience to an innate knowledge of right and wrong are taken together:

> One Word through all things everlastingly,
> One Word – whose voice alas the wicked spurn;
> Insatiate for the good their spirits yearn:
> Yet seeing see not, neither hearing hear
> God's universal law, which those revere
> By reason guided, happiness who win.[5]

Centuries later Marcus Aurelius was saying the same:

> Live with the gods. And he lives with
> the gods whoever presents to them his soul
> accepting their dispensations and busied about
> the will of God, even that particle of Zeus
> which Zeus gives to every man for his controller
> and governor – to wit, his mind and reason.[6]

The philosophical emperor presents a morally sanitized Zeus and it is easy to see how, for Christians, 'particle of [a reformed] Zeus' could become 'particle of the [Judaeo-Christian] God'.

Syneidesis was not a term used by Stoic philosophers, nor was it ever linked to the Stoic 'nature' as *conscientia* had been by Cicero. Its basic meaning was consciousness, perception of one's own thoughts, a 'knowing with' oneself. A. C. Pierce has shown that the main Stoic philosophers never used the term.[7] There is only the fragment, wrongly attributed to Epictetus:

> When we were children our parents handed us over to a nursery slave who should watch over us everywhere lest harm befall us. But when we are grown up, God hands us over to the *syneidesis* implanted in us, to protect us. Let us not in any way despise its protection, for should we do so we will be both ill-pleasing to God and have our *syneidesis* as our enemy.[8]

The classical and koine Greek sense of *syneidesis* is 'conscious self-awareness' and came to have connotations of a sense of the divine by way of perception of an ordered universe. The ancient Greek poet Menander makes this connection in an aphorism where *syneidesis* may, lacking a context, mean either simply consciousness or something closer to

Cicero's *conscientia*, a sense of right and wrong. 'For all mortals *syneidesis* is God'[9] – or vice versa. Liddell and Scott were unable to cite the meaning of moral law except in relation to some ambivalent texts of Biblical Greek: Wisdom 17.11, Acts 23.1, 1 Tim. 3.9.[10] The Wisdom text is particularly difficult: its context is the fear which arises from undetected wickedness: 'For cowardliness (*deinon*) bears witness in its own way in the condemnation of evil, and is always pressing against the rough, being vexed by *syneidesis*'.[11]

Conscience, then, is something which cannot be totally suppressed by the bad man: he has a judge within, which takes the form of a tormenting fear that troubles him: 'Fear arises from nothing other than the additional gift (*prosdosia*), those helps which derive from the reasonable'.[12]

Authoritative translations render *prosdosia* as 'surrender': thus RSV, NRSV and R. H. Charles. I am suggesting a translation which derives directly from the derivative verb *prosdidomi*, which means a 'giving besides'. My point is that fear arises precisely because the innate sense of right and wrong can never be surrendered: if it could the wicked would not be tormented.[13] The New Testament references are easier to translate but much less clearly concerned with a moral sense. In Acts 23, St Paul before the Sanhedrin says 'I have been governed by God until this day by a totally good *syneidesis*' and 1 Tim. 3. refers to 'holding the mystery of faith in a pure *syneidesis*'. In both cases conscience could mean consciousness – of God and his will, rather than an innate moral sense only. In the Pauline writings, of course, *syneidesis* is used in the sense of an innate moral law. His was an original theological contribution. His usage and its interpretation will be discussed as part of the account I shall give of the Scriptural and patristic use of conscience, which form the sources of the Eastern Orthodox tradition. First, however, it is necessary to see how *syneidesis* is used in Eastern Orthodox life itself, what spiritual realities it denotes and how it forms part of the language which characterizes the Eastern Orthodox tradition.

The Orthodox tradition

Orthodoxy, like other Christian denominational groups, identifies the Bible and the Fathers and Mothers of the Church as
its foundation and inspiration. The best place, however, to
gain an understanding of how Eastern Orthodoxy conceives
conscience is the anthology of patristic writings on the inward
life known as the *Philokalia*. The texts may be old but the
volumes themselves were edited and compiled in the age of
the eighteenth-century rationalist Encyclopaedists. Elisabeth
Behr-Sigel has pointed out that, despite the isolation of Mount
Athos, where the *Philokalia* was compiled by Nicodemus of
Naxos and Macarius of Corinth, there were 'subtle links' with
the Enlightenment: 'The idea of gathering together all human
knowledge in a vast encyclopaedia was part of the atmosphere
during the second half of the 18th century'.[14]

However, where the Encyclopaedists concentrated on pointing the torchlight of reason upon the varied aspects of the
external world, the theme of the *Philokalia* is the inward life:
it is the encyclopaedia of the heart. The word *philokalia*
means love of beauty in the Hellenic sense of *kalon k'agathon,*
the beautiful and good. It also had the sense of a collection of
writings, from the fourth-century *Philokalia,* a compilation of
Origen's writings made by St Basil the Great and Gregory
Nazianzen. The Greek Athonite *Philokalia* was published in
Venice in 1782. It became widely influential in the Slavic and
Moldavian region, owing to its translation into Slavonic by the
Ukrainian St Paisius Velickhovsky. This was a selection of
texts from the Greek edition, published in Moscow in 1793,
and reprinted in 1822. Two Russian translations followed, in
1857 and in 1883. An extended Romanian version began to
appear in 1946 and has just been completed. A French edition
is in progress. An English translation of the Greek *Philokalia*
is now available. Moreover, there were works, such as those
by Ignaty Brianchaninov (the 1857 Russian translator), which
epitomised the teaching of the *Philokalia*.[15] There was, too,
the anonymous *Sincere Tales of a Pilgrim to his Spiritual
Father,*[16] published in Kazan in 1884 and in Moscow in 1911.
This lively work, describing the joys and tribulations of a
strannik – a poor wandering pilgrim-peasant – caught the

imagination of East and West and is best known in the English speaking world in the elegant translation of R. M. French. The narrative is vivid and often (probably unintentionally) funny but its theme is the attainment of unceasing prayer. It quotes the *Philokalia* frequently – indeed, it tells the story of how the virtually penniless pilgrim acquires a battered copy from a bookseller. The *Philokalia*, then, represents the modern Eastern Orthodox renaissance of the inner life.

The full title of the Greek *Philokalia* indicates the overarching idea of which conscience is an aspect, namely *nipsis*: 'The Philokalia of the Niptic Holy Ones'. [17]

Nipsis is a very broad term which may be translated as watchfulness. Literally it means the opposite of drunken stupor. It is a spiritual alertness by which one keeps watch over one's inward thoughts. It is, to quote Bishop Kallistos Ware, a term 'used to indicate the whole range of the practice of the virtues'. [18] Two consequences follow from this understanding of the *Philokalia*'s nature and purpose. Firstly, the Greek term 'conscience'/*syneidesis*, in the sense of the voice of God which infallibly tells us right from wrong, is not a key concept for human moral and religious existence, as it is in expositions of western objective intuitionists such as Hutcheson, Butler or Newman. [19] Secondly, conscience is part of a conceptual system to describe ascesis, the spiritual struggle necessary for fellowship with God; it does not have, in the *Philokalia*, the sense of a secular autonomous faculty by which justice may be discerned. Indeed, St Isaac the Syrian, one of the most influential of ascetical writers in eastern Christianity, denies that Christianity is a religion of justice: rather it is one of mercy: 'Do not call God just, for His justice is not manifest in the things concerning you. And if David calls Him just and upright (Ps. 24.8, 144.7), His Son revealed to us that He is good and merciful ... Where is His justice? We were sinners and Christ died for us'. [20]

Although we have seen that natural justice played an important part in Byzantine law, it was and is wholly absent in the Orthodox view of life in Christ. To quote St Isaac the Syrian again: 'Justice does not belong to the Christian way of life and there is no mention of it in Christ's Teaching.' [21] This is a paradox – Byzantine law and the ascetical sense of mercy – to which I will return in the conclusion.

The Orthodox Church's view of conscience, then, is inseparable from its sense of the theological nature of human existence: the invitation to human beings to intimate communion with the Divine Trinity. 'Theology' means prayer in its double aspect of prayer as dogma and dogma as prayer; the spiritualization of dogma and the dogmatization of spirituality. Moreover, human existence is 'theological' in the sense that reasoning about the metaphysical questions of who and what we humans are takes place in Orthodoxy in the arena of an encounter between human lack – the falling short of the glory of God – and the energies of the Trinity. Creation or nature is God's initiative, and, though damaged by the mysterious catastrophe of the Fall, speaks to the now obfuscated sense of the numinous in beings created in the image and likeness of God. Human beings, even without a special revelation, find themselves troubled by the tension they find within of *is* and *ought*; as St Paul puts it, 'their conscience condemning them' (Rom. 2.15). This troubled recognition is the first movement towards the life of grace. St Mark the Ascetic declared that 'the conscience is nature's book' but added immediately afterwards a sentence showing that reading nature's book is being drawn into a living relationship with God, rather than merely having understood moral rules and realized intellectually that God exists, for 'He who applies what he reads there experiences God's help'.[22]

Divine revelation intensifies a divine–human encounter which, through the pricking of conscience (*katanixis* – Acts 2.37), may in the case of some people, already have begun to take place. This special intensification, the divine initiatives of the persons of the Trinity in the lives of the men and women of ancient Israel and in the decisive moment of the incarnation, is life in the Kingdom of God. With life in Christ, conscience forms one element which cannot be separated from the whole ascetical life, which is concerned with awareness and discernment about oneself, a consciousness which may fluctuate between, on the one hand, transfiguration, an experience in this life of Christ's glorification on Mount Thabor, of the uncreated light, and, on the other, a confused entanglement with the passions, the *epithymiai*, some good in themselves but prone to misuse (such as material prosperity, sex, eating and drinking),[23] others invariably evil (pride, love of power, avarice and deliberate systematic voluptuousness).[24] The lover of Christ strives for true discernment (*diakrisis*) and judgement (*dianoia*) about him or herself. It is an understanding of what is obstructing even greater intimacy with God, the barrier of sin. Discernment is not infallible, but a constant mental inquisition has to be held, in order to know what passions need to be controlled or rooted out. At the onset of the spiritual warfare, the ascetic forms a strategy based on self-knowledge, one which must be formed, and re-formed as battles are lost. There is no luminous, self-evident awareness of what is right and wrong in the spiritual life. The human being is, from the start, a mystery to him or herself. This is why in Orthodox prayer books we pray for forgiveness for sins we do not know that we have committed. A rational criticism of this is that we cannot be guilty of what we do not even know we have done – it is just not fair. Orthodoxy, however, is not about freedom from blame in the sense of a consciousness present to one by which one is exonerated – a 'clear conscience'. It is about fellowship with God, rather than morality considered autonomously, and it does not suggest that there is in practice an innate paradigm to which we can have recourse. Like Aquinas, Orthodox realize that, in regard to conscience, we can get it wrong. Unlike Aquinas, Orthodox theology does not proclaim the sovereignty of conscience,[25] because what is truly conscience may not be the conscience of our immediate perception. Conscience, like all other judgements concerning the self, may be obscured. The Orthodox ascetical life is therefore perilous.

The analysis of conscience in the ascetic writings

To present the Orthodox view of conscience in the context of watchfulness and true discernment immerses us in the ontological dimension of religious psychology, the vision of the development of a human being from *prosopic identity*, the face we present to the world, towards *hypostatic identity*, what we really are: 'made in the image and likeness of God'. This very broad understanding of what may be called conscience is the basis of the whole ascetical life. *Syneidesis*, however, is only one term in a whole battery of expressions to convey *nipsis*. *Katanixis* is often used as a term for conscience; it has the sense of 'pricking'. There is a much more important word, which contains a whole theology in itself – *penthos*, traditionally but not very accurately translated as 'compunction': the Latin derivative, *compunctio,* better conveys the 'pricking' of *katanixis. Penthos* means 'mourning'. It is 'a godly sorrow, engendered by repentance; penthos is a feeling accompanied by sadness and suffering because of the privation of what gives joy.'[26]

Thus does Irénée Hausherr SJ choose a definition from the twelfth century *Life of St Cyril of Philea* which accords with his prediliction for scholastic precision. Fr Hausherr points out that the grieving is not tormented but hopeful, quoting St Barsanuphius: 'One must not be saddened by anything in this world'.[27] The learned Jesuit makes what is perhaps a forced antithesis between two terms, *lype* (grief) and *penthos* (mourning). His argument is that the grief referred to as *lype* is a destructive and selfish grief, while the mourning of *penthos* is a divinely-inspired affection, resulting from deep repentance. Hausherr describes *lype* as 'the seed of hell' while *penthos* is the 'fruit of grace' and declares dramatically that to confuse the two is a 'disastrous mistake'.[28] He is confronted with the inconvenient statement of St Paul in 2 Cor. 7.10: 'The *lype* according to God achieves repentance (*metanoia*) for salvation – something not to be repented of'.[29] His answer is to declare that 'the ascetics prefer to give another name to the sadness which is of God. So great a horror have they of the sadness which is of the world'.[30] Such a position has two disadvantages. Firstly, it makes the ascetics sound as if they knew better than St Paul, something quite inconsistent with their reverence for every word of Scripture. Secondly, *lype* and its derivatives are used in a positive sense in the *Philokalia*. For example, St Peter of Damascus (probably eighth century), quoting Dorotheus of Gaza (sixth century), the great popularizer and summarizer of desert asceticism, declares that the first of eight stages of noetic vision is: 'The knowledge of the tribulations of this life and its temptations'.[31] St Peter adds that this knowledge 'grieves (*lypeitai*) all the damage which human nature suffered from sin'.[32] Moreover, St Diodochus of Photike in his century of texts on spiritual knowledge and discrimination says:

> The joy of the one who is starting on the path is other than that of the one made perfect. The first is not exempt from fantasy while the second has the power of humility. But between the two joys comes a sorrow dear to God (*lype theophiles*).* For in being filled with wisdom [Eccles. 1.18] there is fullness of knowledge and he that increases knowledge increases sorrow.[33]
>
> * [Another reading is 'painless weeping' (*lype analgeton*).]

This sorrow, *lype,* now joined to another term *algema* meaning 'pain', continues St Diodoche, has a purifying effect: 'The soul having been tested by the divine reproving (*elenxis*) as in a furnace, it may seize the warm energy of joy without fantasy in remembrance of God'.[34] Grief (*lype*) and pain (*algema*) are regarded positively and related to the metaphor of a furnace for smelting metal (*choneuterion*).[35] There is a reference to the trials of Job and his assertion against his false comforters that the correcting reprisal has come from God, not from human beings – it is the *elenxis* which is not human. (Job 21.17).[36]

Fr Hausherr's tendency to want to establish inappropriately crystalline conceptual distinctions has led to a filtering-out of the richness and nuanced quality of philocalic psychology. *Lype* is the Pauline word for what the ascetics called both *lype* and *penthos*. There is, however, an important qualification to be made between the wrong and right kind of grief. St John Cassian – Cassian the Roman in the Eastern Orthodox tradition – in his *Treatise for Bishop Kastor On the Eight Vices* has a chapter on *lype* (*Peri Lypes*). St John Cassian distinguishes between the despairing grief which leads us away from God, which is a vice, and the kind of grief that is good. The latter is nothing other than the joyful grief of *penthos*. 'The only grief we should practise in asceticism (*askesomen*) is the one which is for repentance of sins, which is accompanied by good hope.'[37] Cassian refers to 2 Cor. 7.10, in which St Paul speaks of the 'sorrow according to God' bringing repentance not to be repented of.

Ascetic consciousness, then, regards *penthos* as a particular kind of grief (*lype*) which leads to *metanoia*. Yet again Hausherr forces an altogether too hard distinction between *penthos* and *metanoia*. The latter term in the English translation is confusingly referred to both as penance and repentance: 'One must be careful not to confuse compunction with penance'.[38]

Having himself confused *metanoia* by using two western terms which have different nuances, Fr Hausherr himself makes it clear that his own sharp separation of *metanoia* and *penthos* cannot be maintained, when he says of St Mark the Ascetic that in discussing *metanoia* the saint 'might have done better to distinguish repentance from *penthos*'. He prefers John Climacus because in his *Ladder of Divine Ascent* this saint gives separate chapters to *metanoia* and *penthos*. It is not clear to me that separation of chapters means total conceptual separation. The *Philokalia* has a different taxonomy from Roman Catholic manuals on the spiritual life. In any case, St John Climacus mentions *metanoia* in his chapter on *penthos*.[39] A reading of St Mark the Ascetic's *On Repentance* shows how *metanoia* has an eschatological reality because the New Testament relates *metanoia* to the Kingdom of Heaven. It is a process of growth: St Mark relates *metanoia* to the parable of the mustard seed.[40] The relationship between the two ideas may be regarded as subtler than as Hausherr presents it: while *metanoia* represents the ascetic consciousness in terms of continual repentance in the already-inaugurated eschaton, *penthos* reflects another aspect of the same consciousness, the purification which the gift of tears can bring and which spurs us on to ever deeper *metanoia*. St Isaac the Syrian makes this very clear:

> Many show an appearance of repentance but no one truly possesses it except the one who is sorely afflicted in his heart. Many run to find compunction of heart but no one finds it is very true save the one who possesses unremitting silence. Everyone who is a servant of God loves compunction. Know that every loquacious person is inwardly empty, though he discourses on amazing things. Inward sorrow is a bridle for the senses. If you love the truth, love silence. This will make you illumined in God like the sun and will deliver you from the illusions of ignorance. Silence unites you to God Himself.[41]

St Isaac joins his discussion of compunction with another important idea, *hesychia*, stillness, silence or quietness, a constant attention to God as found in the centre of the human being – in the heart. His discussion balances the idea of stillness with warmly affective language, quoting Evagrius of Pontus, the fourth-century philosopher-monk and Origenist:

> As Abba Evagrius says 'Fervent compunction is a purifying herb; through the holy angels the Lord gives it for diligent cleansing of passions to those who repent'. And again he says 'Fervent compunction of soul is the fire of a furnace that by Christ's grace comes upon the soul at the time of prayer and thereupon the faculty of recollection attains to divine vision.'[42]

This purification from passion is quite different, then, from the cold detachment (*ataraxia*) of Stoicism.

To sum up so far, in Orthodoxy conscience may be very broadly understood as the consciousness of God, *nipsis*, which is described with subtle psychology by terms which are interwoven with one another. *Metanoia* is a constant changing of attitude, accompanied by the purification of the gift of tears, a 'godly grief' (*kata theon lype*) or *penthos*. Another way of describing *penthos* is *katanixis,* a pricking. The ascetic life strives for inner stillness and silence, *hesychia*, and attention to the heart and has always to be attended by discrimination (*diakrisis*) and right judgement (*dianoia agathe*), in the uneven journey towards deification (*theosis, theopoiesis*).

It remains to consider how the narrower sense of conscience as *syneidesis* is used in ascetical language. Not surprisingly *syneidesis* does not necessarily mean a moral arbiter. Characteristic is St Philotheus of Sinai's teaching, where *syneidesis* is discussed in the context of purity of heart and *katanixis*. 'Let us preserve our heart's purity and always be filled with compunction towards God through this best of understandings.'[43]

Syneidesis is awareness found in prayer and is part of the 'Royal Way': first, reading Scripture day and night in stillness (*hesychia*); secondly, being tested in all things by *syneidesis*; thirdly, awe of God; fourthly, compunction (inward grief), and finally, the spirit of martyrdom and self-sacrifice. This is the joyful road of dispassion (*apatheia*) and spiritual knowledge.[44] The 'way' is nothing other than Christianity itself. Elsewhere St Philotheus presents *syneidesis* as the 'soul's mirror',[45] which watchfulness cleanses. This is a very important point about the inward awareness of God denoted by *syneidesis*: conscience can be obscured; it leads only to knowledge of God 'when purified through active, applied and meticulous watchfulness of the intellect'.[46] St Philotheus sees *syneidesis* as a way of describing *nipsis*. Similarly, St Peter of Damascus refers to the 'natural knowledge given to us by God'.[47] This is *syneidesis* which is the starting point of the spiritual life. We can come to *syneidesis* by different routes, such as Scripture or by the angel in baptism.

Syneidesis does also have a sense of judgement of right and wrong. This is most discussed in St Maximus Confessor's *Second Century on Love* as part of his account of 'noetic discrimination which distinguishes the external and transitory'. The 'persuasion' of *syneidesis* towards evil can take place but it has disastrous consequences:

> He who persuades his conscience to regard the evil he is doing as good by nature reaches out with his moral faculty in a reprehensible manner; for he thinks that what is thoroughly evil is by nature immortal. Therefore God, who has implanted in human conscience a natural hatred of evil, cuts him off from life, for he has now become evil in his will and intention. God acts in this way so that when a human being does wrong he cannot persuade his own conscience that what is thoroughly evil is good by nature.[48]

Here, then, there is the belief in a moral sense which cannot be ignored. It should, however, be noted that St Maximus contextualizes his account in relation to the Fall, the wrong reaching out for the tree of life, a deliberate murder, as it were, of conscience by a substitution of evil for good resulting in expulsion from Paradise. St Maximus presents the Fall not as an historical event so much as a perpetual tendency by which we might lose fellowship with God.

Dorotheus of Gaza wrote a chapter on conscience which clearly has a threefold moral sense: behaviour towards God, one's neighbour and oneself. There are sentences such as the following, which make conscience into an irrefragable moral faculty: 'No one is without a conscience, since it is something divinely implanted in us ... and it can never be destroyed'.[49] However, the opening to this very chapter describes conscience as a divine energy: 'When God created man, he breathed into him something divine, as it were a hot and bright spark added to reason, which lit up the mind and showed him the difference between right and wrong'.[50] Yet it became 'buried and trodden underfoot',[51] a buried spark. Divine revelation, first in the law and the prophets, and finally, in Jesus Christ, resurrected it, 'so that is [again] in our power either to bury it again, or, if we obey it, to allow it to shine out and illuminate us'.[52] It is Dorotheus' teaching on *syneidesis* which epitomizes the Eastern Orthodox position: conscience is an originally innate capacity to judge of good and evil, which in the context of fallen human nature has been obscured and which requires the divine *Logos* to uncover it. Even after the acceptance of faith, *syneidesis* can become opaque again, so that the life of faith is a continual fall–redemption–death–resurrection drama rather than a definable moment.

Ecumenicity and particularism in Orthodox thought

Twentieth-century Orthodox who comment upon ethics have come to some distorted conclusions precisely because of the theological nature of conscience, broadly or narrowly understood. Sergius Bulgakov stated forthrightly: 'Orthodoxy knows no such thing as "autonomous ethic"' which, he suggests, forms the special spiritual gift of Protestantism. For Orthodoxy, ethics is religious: it is the image of the salvation in the soul.[53] It follows for him that the 'monastic ideal'[54] – what I would call the ascetic tradition – is for all. Vassilios Giultsis identifies ethics with dogma. By dogma he means a mystical living out of the Church's teaching, in liturgy and prayer. Orthodoxy's 'ethical attitude' consists of 'faith and piety, theology and life constituting an indissoluble unity in which the virtues are experienced as "fruits of the spirit"'. [55]

It is a short step to ecclesiastical triumphalism. Thus, Jerome Kotsonis states: 'It is certainly a fact that the foundations of Orthodox ethics differ from those of other Christian confessions.'[56] Kotsonis gives short shrift to those outside the Orthodox Church: 'although the Church does not consider the person who has not been illuminated by the light of faith as wholly irresponsible and entirely incapable of truth and perceiving the good, yet it does not look upon him with much sympathy'.[57]

More recently Stanley S. Harakas, in his *Contemporary Moral Issues Facing the Orthodox Christian*, has attempted to redress the balance by reminding us that ethical issues challenge Orthodox people in the contemporary world. He attempts a sensitive and provisional overview. Yet the book draws upon Orthodox tradition piecemeal rather than uncovering the deeper issues about conscience. His book sometimes gives the impression of providing a check list of what you can, or cannot, get away with in the Orthodox Churches in the United States of America.[58]

It is Christos Yannaras who identifies, in twentieth-century terms, the nature of the ethical in Orthodoxy in a way which exposes the crudity we have seen above. Yannaras rejects 'morality' as an 'objective' yardstick for evaluating the individual character or behaviour. Such an ethic, he argues, 'separates the ethos or morality of man, his individual behaviour, from his existential truth and hypostatic identity – from what man *is* prior to any social or objective evaluation of him'. [59] Yannaras is, in the Heideggerian sense, 'existential' in his approach, in that existence precedes essence. Hypostatic identity, being made in God's image and likeness, is coupled with a human person's existential truth. The ontology of ethics is manifested only existentially. This understanding of ethics, it seems to me, agrees with the ancient material I have discussed. Firstly, the terminology describes human existentiality: this is why terms overlap and are interwoven. The ascetics discuss the unfolding of consciousness of God, and of the *syneidesis* of right and wrong, of how the mirror shines or how its reflection is obscured, in personal terms. Truth is subjective not, in the sense that the being of God or moral truths depend on personal quirks, but in the sense that such truths are realized in subjects as part of a relationship to God.

This approach towards conscience avoids narrow sectarianism and legalism. This is the view that the institutional church knows the rules and dictates to its members, without there being a necessity for the person concerned to search his heart or exercise his mind, as outsiders would have to: right and wrong are essentially what you are *told*. This authoritarian externalism provokes so often the conflict between external authority and inward conscience. Yannaras also avoids the extreme of asserting that moral rules emanate from an inexplicable sense of presence, sometimes called mystical, from which the non-Christian or even the wrong kind of Christian is excluded, and by which moral *reasoning* is impossible as a canonical member of the Orthodox Church.

I argue that the Orthodox tradition has every sympathy with what Kotsonis calls 'the person who has not been illuminated by the light of faith', if their moral searching is thoughtful and serious. Byzantium had its day as a state, and it may be argued that Justinian's systematization of Roman law codes on Stoic lines was a totalization at a time when the Empire was in trouble. It took a long time but Byzantium did fall. But long before the Turks finally breached its walls there had emerged an ascetical tradition typified in the monk, but also found in laypersons,[60] and even kings,[61] which resisted such totalization and pointed to the hidden *noesis*, potentially transfiguring but often refracted. The ascetical tradition presents a form of reasoning, although it is not a rationalized ethical theory in terms of western philosophy. It dissects human existentiality and points to the tragedy of a buried or murdered conscience – our blindness to reality. The ascetics make it perfectly clear that church membership alone cannot resurrect conscience, and the Byzantine Niptic Fathers did well to do so in a world where Byzantine identity and Orthodox Church membership were conflated in such a way as to amount to nominal Christianity. Their protest can be heard again when particular expressions of Eastern Orthodox Christianity become aspects of nationalism and ethnicity. St Paul addressed 'the person who has not been illuminated by the light of faith', to return to Kotsonis' phrase, in terms of a *syneidesis* of right and wrong. The discussion is part of his presentation of natural knowledge of God through the world's order, which has been obscured, leading to all kinds of misery and misery-making (Rom. 1.19–20). St Athanasius in his *Contra Gentes* calls this natural knowledge as arising from the *dianoia* or innate judgement in human beings. Existentially, however, this knowledge (*gnorisma*)[62] has been veiled and the *homoiosis*[63] or likeness to God obscured, so that there is no longer a 'hearing' of God (*akoue*).[64] To humans in their present condition, there is lost 'the vision of intelligible reality'.[65] Athanasius is only 'against' the 'gentiles' or pagans in that he is persuading them, urging them on to find again their vision in the revelation of the *Logos*: 'For just as light is good and better is the sun, the originator of life, so once the divine creation existed it was necessary that all humanity should be filled with knowledge of him, knowledge that he is the originator and ruler of this successful project, namely God and God the Word'.[66] In his sequel, the *De Incarnatione*, Athanasius explains the salvific initiative, in terms of sympathy towards human beings now blinded by passion, and having lost the clear vision of being. 'Hence the Word of God arrived by his own agency in order that he might have the power to revive the human being who is according to the image.'[67]

Noetic and physical resurrection are taken together, just as are noetic blindness and physical death. Rather than adopting a strictly rationalist proof, which can convince with apodeictic certainty, Athanasius deliberately deploys rhetoric to persuade *persons*. To put it another way, his thought has a kerygmatic structure. While he did not explain the mystery of human freedom – and perhaps did not choose to – he at least came to terms with it, by demonstrating, existentially, the need for commitment. He shows that human beings have the potential for tragedy and despair on the one hand and, on the other, for a rediscovery of the worth of the human person in a world manifesting itself as absurd. The Orthodox ascetics take Athanasius' theology further: noetic blindness and its resurrection in the restoration of conscience, its potential loss and the flashes of insight which again restore it, is a perpetual issue not only for the unbaptized but for the baptized as well.

Athanasius' sympathy for gentile and Jew has a fierce and possessive quality. His zealous persuasion derives its urgency from his conviction that those who do not accept help from the divine *Logos* are doomed. The strength of his antipathy towards those who remained Jews while the gospel was being proclaimed is demonstrated by his description of Arianism, the heresy he hated so much and spent a lifetime fighting, as renewed Judaism, and by his comparison of the manner of Arius's death with the fate of Judas.[68] Similarly, the outcome for those who remain pagans is luridly described as a total fall into spiritual blindness and deafness, the symptoms of which are disgusting – the proliferation of idolatry and debauchery.[69] The question, however, remains as to the teaching of Orthodoxy as a whole, for the teaching of one Father, no matter how great has to be balanced by the teaching of other saints, theologians and ascetics. Are, then, those who, in the end, remain Jews or pagans off the map of conscience, as St Athanasius appears to suggest?

There are, in fact, other readings of the first two chapters of St Paul's Letter to the Romans amongst the Fathers. St John Chrysostom, one of the Three Great Hierarchs of Orthodoxy,[70] and the normative interpreter of Scripture, argues that those who, amongst Jews and gentiles, have not accepted the gospel may or may not be 'inexcusable' (Rom. 2.1), depending upon their response to the natural knowledge of God and his will. God has established an imprint of himself in Creation. Here Chrysostom quotes Rom. 1.20: 'the invisible things of [God] are clearly seen from the creation of the world, being understood by the things which are made'. Commenting on this, Chrysostom implies that the minds of the gentiles are not so darkened as in practice to be unable to live a godly and virtuous life. Here, Chrysostom is optimistic about human possibilities outside Christianity: 'for it was not to bereave them of all excuse, that God set before them so great a system of teaching, but that they might come to know Him'.[71] Their inexcusability consists of turning towards idols through 'having some great conceit of themselves'.[72] Their fault lies not in failing to receive Christ, but in doing what is innately wrong: worshipping creation, rather than the Creator. Chrysostom does not mention the Jews here, but there is a clear inference to be drawn: if rejection of idolatry puts you on God's side, then the Jews are as much on God's side as the gentiles who find God in Creation.

Later in his commentary on Romans, in relation to chapter

2, Chrysostom considers gentiles and Jews together. He is discussing verse 15: '[The gentiles] show the work of the law written on their hearts, their conscience also bearing witness, and their thoughts the meanwhile accusing or else excusing them'. Chrysostom remarks: 'Those were to be the rather honoured who without the Law strove earnestly to fulfil the things of the Law.'[73] The natural law and its equivalent, the Jewish Law, are honourable. Chrysostom favours the gentile over the Jew – 'the gentile is greater than the Jew'[74] – because, we must suppose, if he does God's will he does so without the benefit of a specific revelation. However, Chrysostom appreciates St Paul's 'discretion'[75] regarding the Jew: St Paul does not *say* 'the gentile is greater than the Jew', in order that 'at least the Jew might receive what is said'.[76] What is it then that the Jew must receive? Chrysostom's point is that 'conscience and reason suffice in the Law's stead',[77] and that, further, conscience derived from innate reason is primordial, for 'Before the Law was given, human nature fully enjoyed the care of providence ... and they knew what was good and what bad'. For Chrysostom, then, the Jewish Law is a re-publication of the natural law in a specific cultural and historical context.[78] For Chrysostom it was always the case that, through conscience 'God made Man independent so as to be able to choose virtue and avoid vice'. Chrysostom, unlike Athanasius, teaches that human beings, even after the Fall, are not so damaged as not to be able to make moral choices by means of innate conscience. The Jew who obeys the Law is worthy of respect in that he or she fulfils the natural law of reason throught the revealed Law. Chrysostom does not demonize Jew or gentile. However, the problem with his position is that he fails to come to terms with the idea that the Jewish Law reveals more to us about God than reason could ever tell us.

Athanasius versus Chrysostom! How is one to decide which understanding of conscience is Orthodox? The characteristic attitude of Orthodoxy is to see both positions as mutually modifying and correcting one another. It is precisely this approach that Dimitriu Staniloae adopts in his *Dogmatic Theology*:

'God reveals himself objectively through conscience and nature. Subjectively, however, on account of the sin within them that they have seconded with their own will, most people either resist the self-evidence of God and of the true meaning of their lives which is revealed to us naturally, or else distort this evidence and refuse to make a contribution of their will necessary to accept it. In a general way Saint Paul attests both these things: the fact of an objective natural revelation in nature and the subjective refusal of many to accept the evidence of God revealed in this way.'[79]

Such an approach may be criticized as vague or as leaving the question as open as possible. People are different and it is hard always to know why: this much the *Philokalia* teaches. It is true of Orthodox Christians and those who are not Christians. Conscience is a general reality, yet for all sorts of reasons it may be obscured in practice. An Orthodox Christian may be no safer than a Jew or a pagan – and perhaps considerably less so[80] – simply by being canonically Orthodox. It was for this very reason that the corpus of ascetical writings grew and that the Orthodox Church urges its people towards constant watchfulness and spiritual activity.[81]

It is because Dostoievski was so well-versed in the *Philokalia* that he was both an Orthodox theologian and a writer of universal appeal, one who inspired both Albert Camus and Karl Barth. In Dostoievski we are plunged into a world where moral conventions are confounded because it is so difficult to see, in these terms, who is good or bad, and because goodness and godliness are to be found in unlikely persons. He analyses human life, not in ethical categories, but in terms of sin and forgiveness, and of insight and insane blindness. Underlying his very modern narrative methods are ancient Christian ascetic ways of describing the human condition. His genius was to present his message existentially, as did the Niptic Fathers, but in a way that can appeal to the modern and contemporary, in narratives that defy rational analysis. In *Crime and Punishment*, Raskolnikov commits a brutal murder, yet the chief of police who suspects him does not arrest him immediately but lets his conscience surface in freedom. When in Siberia, he is confined yet free, and his final thoughts are not of conversion to church affiliation, even though he has the New

Testament under his pillow, but of whether or not he can share the life of the paradoxically saintly prostitute Sonia, who has loved him so much. In *The Possessed* Stepan Verkhovensky finally intuits, from the necessity of his own personal love for God, God's *reality*. Dostoievski's ontology and his existentiality are one as he presents tragedy and redemption in terms of personal consciences distorted and obscured by obsessive passion and restored by personal love. So many people from every faith and none have read, re-read and loved Dostoievski's works because he expands the consciousness of human spirituality more widely than any novelist, by the subtlety of his psychology and the breadth of his vision. The Eastern Orthodox ascetic writers I have used, sometimes aphoristic, sometimes crabbed, yet sometimes using images of extraordinary beauty, are attempting the same. If they helped to produce a Dostoievski, I would argue that in themselves they still have much to say about conscience to our own age.

If Dostoievski's philocalic modernity has its intensity and complexity to offer to the issue of conscience, it is an ancient, St Isaac of Nineveh, who offers fragrance and simplicity. Out of his concern with purity of heart and stillness, there arises a way of looking at conscience, which, while not neglecting Greek philosophical precision,[82] uses semitic and biblical images. Isaac discerns a close relation between conscience, the Holy Spirit, mercy, and immersion in the Holy Scriptures:

> One who reads great works in an ordinary way profanes his heart, depriving it of that holy power which gives it a sweet taste with meanings which fill the soul with wonder. All things run towards their likeness. And the soul in which there is a portion of the spirit when it learns something with a spiritual power hidden in it, ardently draws out the story.[83]

There is great hope in his message. The reference to the 'portion of the spirit' is a reference to Wisd. 12.1. [84] St Isaac interprets the passage as meaning that there is an indestructible element within us – even as we sin – which will lead us back into the redemptive story of scriptural narration. I suggest a merciful and hopeful translation of this passage intended in the spirit of St Isaac of Nineveh: 'Your indestructible spirit is in all. So, a little at a time, you convince those who have fallen by the wayside, and, in the case of those who are still making mistakes, you restore their memory and advise them, in order that, escaping from evil, they may trust in you, O Lord.'

For 'chasteneth' (Lancelot Brenton), or 'correctest' (RSV), I advocate 'convince', from the idea of *elenxis* as a refutation in rational argument. For 'that offend' (Brenton), or 'those who trespass' (RSV), I suggest the idea of mistake, since the Greek *hamartia* means literally 'to err', or 'to fall short of a target'. For 'warnest' (Brenton) and RSV 'warn' , I render 'advise'. Since the Greek is *noutheteis*, I have chosen a less threatening translation than 'warn', taken from the roots *nous* (mind) and *tithemi* (to place). For 'remind', I render 'restore their memory', because *hypomimneskon* is an intensive form of *mimnesko*, to remind. For 'leaving their wickedness' (Brenton) or 'may be freed' (RSV) I advocate the stronger sense of 'escape'. For the cliched 'believe' (Brenton), I prefer the RSV 'put their trust in', which keeps the literal Greek sense of *pisteuo*. I offer a translation inspired by the reading of a Father imbued with mercy and hope. While much in the philocalic tradition rightly emphasizes the difficulties of conscience, I believe it right to conclude on such a note. I therefore end with the prayer with which every Orthodox Christian begins his other prayers, in Morning Prayer, Evening Prayer and at Holy Liturgy. There is a sense in which it is a prayer about conscience:

> O Heavenly King, the Comforter, the Spirit of truth who art everywhere present and fillest all things, treasury of good and giver of life, come and abide in us and purify us from every impurity and save, O Gracious One, our souls.

Notes

1   Cicero, *De Re Publica*, III, xii, 33.
2   A. P. d'Entrives, *Natural Law* (Hutchinson University Library, London, 1967), p. 25.
3   loc.cit.
4   F. Coplestone, SJ, *History of Philosophy* (Search Press, London, 1946).

5   ET of James Adam (1910), cited in Coplestone, op. cit., p. 393.
6   Coplestone, p. 437.
7   A. C. Pierce, *Conscience in the New Testament* (SCM Press, London, 1958), p. 13.
8   ibid., p. 51
9   Liddell and Scott, *A Greek–English Lexicon* (Clarendon Press, Oxford, 1891), p. 13.
10 loc. cit.
11 My translation, from the Greek of ed. Alfred Rahlfs, Septuaginta (Württembergisch Bibelanstalt, Stuttgart, 1935), p. 372. The RSV has 'For wickedness is a cowardly thing, condemned by its own testimony; distressed by conscience, it has always exaggerated the difficulties' – a rather conjectural translation of a passage which is possibly textually corrupt, aiming at readability, see H. G. May and B. M. Metzger, The New Oxford Annotated Bible with Apocrypha (Oxford University Press, Oxford, 1977), p. 124. The NRVS (1989) retains this translation.
12 *Septuaginta*, p. 372.
13 R. H. Charles, *The Apocrypha and Pseudepigrapha of the Old Testament in English* (Clarendon Press, Oxford, 1913). Charles remarks that this passage is the first occurrence in the Bible of an idea of conscience.
14 E. Behr-Sigel, *The Place of the Heart. An Introduction to Orthodox Spirituality*, (Oakwood Publications, Torrance, California, 1992), p. 105.
15 Available in ET are *The Arena*, tr. Archimandrite Lazarus (Holy Trinity Monastery, Jordanville, New York, 1991), and *On the Prayer of Jesus*, tr. Father Lazarus, (Element Books, Shaftesbury, Dorset, 1993).
16 tr. R. M. French, *The Way of a Pilgrim* (SPCK, London, 1972) and *The Pilgrim Continues His Way* (SPCK, London, 1973).
17 There is a reproduction of the 1782 Venice edition title page in ed. E. Kadloubovsky and G. E. H. Palmer, *Writings from the Philokalia on Prayer of the Heart*, (Faber & Faber, London, 1951, 9th impression, 1977), p. 8. The first four words of the very long title are: *philokalia ton ieron niptikon*.
18 tr. and ed. G. E. H. Palmer, P. Sherrard and Kallistos Ware, *The Philokalia. The Complete Text*, (Faber & Faber, London, 1979), p. 367 (Glossary). The glossary is a very valuable key to the terminology used in the *Philokalia*.
19 *New Encyclopaedia Britannica, Micropaedia* (Chicago University Press, 1988, p. 551: intuitionism is 'the view that

holds conscience to be an innate faculty determining the perception of right and wrong'. See also ed. T. Honderich, *The Oxford Companion to Philosophy* (Oxford University Press, Oxford, 1995), p. 152. In Butler conscience is the voice of God. It is 'infallible and generally philanthropic', 'inviolate', M. Eliade, Encyclopaedia of Religion, IV (Macmillan, New York, 1987), p. 49.

20 Isaac the Syrian, *The Ascetical Homilies*, tr. Holy Transfiguration Monastery, (Holy Transfiguration Monastery, Boston, MA, 1984), pp. 250–1.This idea lived on into the forests of nineteenth-century Russia. St Seraphim of Sarov quotes the very same passage of St Isaac in his *Spiritual Instruction, Little Russian Philokalia* (St Herman Press, New Valaam, Alaska), p. 25.

21 St Isaac, *Ascetical Homilies*, p. 246.

22 ed. Ware et al., Mark the Ascetic, *The Philocalia. The Complete Text*, I, p. 123.

23 St Isaac the Syrian, *On Ascetical Life*, tr. Mary Hansbury, (St Vladimir's Press, Crestwood, New York, 1989), p. 81: 'Occasions for sin are wine and women, riches and a healthy body. It is not that these things are to be designated as sin, but on account of human weakness and the unlawful use of them.' Bishop Kallistos Ware observes a difference of opinion about the passions amongst the philocalic writers: while some, such as St John Climacus, see all passions as evil, others such, for example, Isaiah the Solitary, see passions as bad only when put to bad use, *Philokalia. Complete Text, I,* p. 363. One must add to that view that St Isaac the Syrian takes a middle line: some passions as essentially bad, and others essentially good, if liable to distortion, see n. 24, below.

24 St Isaac, *On Ascetical Life,* p. 40, lists the intrinsically bad passions: 'Love of riches; amassing possessions; the fattening of the body, which proceeds from carnal desire; love of honours, which is the source of envy; administration of government; pride and pomp of power; elegance; popularity which is the cause of ill-will; fear for the body.'

25 Eliade, op. cit., p. 46.

26 I. Hausherr SJ, *Penthos. The Doctrine of Compunction in the Christian East*, tr. Anselm Hufstader, OSB, (Cistercian Publications, Kalamazoo, Michigan, 1982). Originally published in French in 1944), p. 4.

27 ibid., p. 4.

28 loc. cit.

29 *he kata theon lype.* RSV translates 'godly grief'.
30 Hausherr, op. cit., p. 4
31 tr. G. E. H. Palmer, P. Sherrard and Kallistos Ware, *The Philokalia. The Complete Text,* III (Faber & Faber, London, 1984), p. 108.
32 *Philokalia,* [Greek Text], Tomos A, (Aster, Athens, 1961), p. 32, reading *lypeitai* as the middle voice – 'grieves on one's own part'.
33 *Philokalia,* [Greek Text], Diodochus of Photike, *Treatise on Spiritual Perfection,* sec. 60; tr. Ware et al., *The Philokalia. The Complete Text,* p. 271 [tr. Ware, modified].
34 loc. cit.
35 *choneuterion* means a furnace for purifying metal.
36 In Ps. 38.12 (Septuagint), the Greek word is used in relation to rebuking or chastening a person for his or her iniquity. However, in Job 21.4 (LXX), the righteous Job declares to his false comforters that the *elenxis* he has received in his suffering is divine, not human: the meaning of the word can be 'refutation', and the passage may be interpreted as meaning that God's mysterious ways confound our human understanding.
37 My translation, from *Philokalia,* (Greek Text), Tomos A, p. 74. tr. Ware et al., *The Philokalia. The Complete Text,* p. 88, has 'The only form of dejection we should cultivate is the sorrow which goes with repentance and is accompanied by hope in God'.
38 Hausherr, op. cit., p. 18.
39 St John Climacus, *The Ladder of Divine Ascent* (Holy Transfiguration Monastery, Boston, MA, 1991), p. 70.
40 This text is not in the *Philokalia* and does not exist in ET. An unreliable Greek text is to be found in ed. Migne, *Patrologia Graeca,* lxv. There is, however, a French translation of a critical text, tr. Soeur Claire-Agnes Zirnheld, OCSO., *Marc le Moine. Traites Spirituels et Théologiques* (Abbaye de Bellefontaine, Begrolles-Manges, 1985), pp. 72–90.
41 St Isaac the Syrian, *Ascetical Homilies,* p. 307.
42 ibid., p. 306.
43 ed Ware et al., *The Philokalia. The Complete Text,* III, p. 30.
44 ibid., p. 88.
45 ibid., p. 25.
46 ibid., p. 27.
47 ibid., p. 76.
48 tr. Ware et al., *Philokalia,* p. 95.
49 Dorotheus of Gaza, *Discourses and Sayings. Desert Humour*

and   Humility tr.   E.P.Wheeler   (Cistercian   Publications, Kalamazoo), Discourse III, 'On Conscience', p. 105.

50 ibid., p. 104.

51 loc. cit.

52 loc. cit.

53 Sergius Bulgakov, *The Orthodox Church*, (Centenary Press, London, 1935), p. 177.

54 *ibid.*, p. 178.

55 V. Giultsis, 'An Ethical Approach to Justice and Peace', in ed. G. Limouris, *Justice and Peace and the Integrity of Orthodoxy*, (Geneva, WCC Publications, 1990), p. 57.

56 J. Kotsonis, 'Fundamental Principles of Orthodox Morality', in ed. A. J. Philippou, *The Orthodox Ethos*, (Holywell Press, Oxford, 1964), p. 229.

57 ibid., p. 231.

58 S. S. Harakas, *Contemporary Moral Issues Facing Orthodox Christians* (Life and Light Publications, Minneapolis, Minnesota, 1982).

59 C. Yannaras, *The Freedom of Morality*, tr. E. Briere, (St Vladimir's Seminary Press, Crestwood, New York, 1984).

60 Nicholas Cabasilas (14th cent.) spent most of his life in the imperial diplomatic service, only later retiring to a monastery where he wrote *The Life in Christ* and *A Commentary on the Divine Liturgy*.

61 For example St Sava, prince, warrior and hesychast monk. See N. Velimerovitch, *The Life of St Sava*, (St Vladimir's Seminary Press, Crestwood, New York, 1989).

62 Athanasius, *Contra Gentes* and *De Incarnatione,* ed. and tr. R. W. Thomson (Clarendon Press, Oxford, 1971), p. 10.

63 ibid., p. 7.

64 ibid., p. 13.

65 ibid., p. 10: *'theoria ton noeton'*

66 ibid., p. 19.

67 ibid., p. 167, my translation.

68 *Epistola ad Serapion de Morte Arii*, Migne *Patrologia Graeca, Works of Athanasius, col. 689, section 5.*

69 Thomson, op. cit., pp. 23–39.

70 The others are Gregory the Theologian (Nazianzen), and Basil the Great, bishop of Caesarea.

71 ed. P. Schaff and H. Wace, *A Select Library of Nicene & Post Nicene Fathers of the Christian* Church (Eerdmans, Michigan, 1976), referred to as NPNF, on Rom. 1.20.

72 On Rom. 1.22.

73 On Rom. 2.11.
74 loc. cit.
75 loc. cit.
76 loc. cit.
77 loc. cit.
78 This resembles the 18th cent. Deists, such as John Toland and Matthew Tindal, who denied that we learn anything new to reason in the Bible. Chrysostom certainly seems to be saying this about the OT.
79 D. Staniloae, *The Experience of God*, tr. I. Ionita and R. Barringer (Holy Cross Orthodox Press, Brookline, MA, 1994), p. 18.
80 'To whom much is given, much will be required.' (Luke 12.48.)
81 In the Orthodox Morning Prayers, the faithful pray to be 'watchful, upright and active' (Prayer of St Basil the Great).
82 St Isaac frequently quotes the philosopher-ascetic Evagrius, a follower of Origen's thought. Isaac too was Origenistic, because the East Syrian (or so-called 'Nestorian') Church was unaffected by the Fifth Ecumenical Council which condemned Origenism.
83 Isaac, *On Ascetical Life*, p. 29.
84 *Septuaginta*, pp. 361–362.

Part Two

5

Conscience in Jewish Tradition

Jonathan Gorsky

Biblical echoes

When the biblical Joseph was tempted by the wife of Potiphar, the text records that he hesitated before finally refusing her advances.[1] A rabbinic gloss indicates that he was about to succumb and was only forestalled by a sudden vision of his father's countenance.[2] Conscience presented itself as an image of his father's face; past associations and memories had a powerful effect upon his behaviour. Joseph had grown up in a religious world: the images he internalized in his formative years were sharply evoked when he found himself in a radically different environment as a young man.[3]

A modern rabbinic authority, Rabbi J. B. Soloveitchik, makes striking use of a second biblical narrative to illustrate the power of conscience. In the first book of Samuel we read of a wealthy man called Nabal who refused to provide sustenance for the future King David and his entourage. David was then an outlaw, in flight from the wrath of King Saul, together with his men. Nabal, who is described as churlish and evil, would have incurred retribution from David if not for the fortunate intervention of his wife Abigail, who provided food and drink for the hungry fugitives. That evening following his refusal Nabal held a drunken banquet. The morning after

Abigail addressed him: 'But it came to pass in the morning, when the wine was gone out of Nabal, and his wife told him these things, that his heart died within him, and he became as a stone.'[4] For R. Soloveitchik, Abigail personifies the voice of conscience.[5]

R. Soloveitchik was drawing on a particular verbal association. The Hebrew Bible has no word for 'conscience': the phenomenon is seen as one of the many promptings of the human heart. When David commits an act of *lèse-majesté* by cutting off a corner of the garment of the sleeping King Saul, he is stricken by conscience: 'And it came to pass afterward, that David's heart smote him, because he had cut off Saul's skirt. And he said unto his men, The Lord forbid, that I should do this thing unto my master, the Lord's anointed, to stretch forth mine hand against him, seeing he is the anointed of the Lord.'[6] A second incident is recorded in a later narrative. David took a census of the people in a manner that was evidently sinful: 'And David's heart smote him after that he had numbered the people. And David said unto the Lord, I have sinned greatly in that I have done; and now, I beseech thee, O Lord, take away the iniquity of thy servant; for I have done very foolishly.'[7]

But the promptings of the heart are innately untrustworthy. Rabbinic introspection is much influenced by the pessimistic statements in the early chapters of Genesis. In the first, the Lord sees the wickedness of humanity and notes that all day evil thoughts proceed from the imaginings of the heart. In the second, at the end of the Flood story, God says to himself: 'I will not again curse the ground any more for man's sake: for the imagination of man's heart is evil from his youth; neither will I again smite any more every thing living, as I have done'.[8] In Numbers, the people are warned categorically not to 'seek ... after your own heart and your own eyes, after which you use to go a whoring',[9] and in Deuteronomy they are told that idolatry is a consequence of the heart's being deceived.[10] As the author of Ecclesiastes puts it, God indeed made humanity 'upright', but people seek out many inventions.[11]

Some biblical writings envisage the prospect of the heart serving as a reliable source of moral guidance. David exhorts his son Solomon to serve God with a 'perfect heart and with a willing mind'.[12] He prays that God will guard the thoughts of Israel's imagination and 'give unto Solomon my son a perfect heart, to keep thy commandments ...'[13] Solomon himself prays for 'an understanding heart to judge thy people, that I may discern between good and bad ...'[14] and his request is granted: 'Behold, I have done according to thy words: lo, I have given thee a wise and an understanding heart, so that there was none like thee before thee, neither after thee shall any arise like unto thee'.[15]

Solomon's innate discernment was a unique divine dispensation, but the prophet Jeremiah, in a famous passage, anticipates that days will come when the promptings of the heart will be dramatically transformed: 'Behold, the days come, saith the Lord, that I will make a new covenant with the house of Israel, and with the house of Judah ... I will put my law [Torah] in their inward parts and write it in their hearts; and will be their God, and they shall be my people'.[16] Knowledge of God will be a common property of the inner life, rather than a lesson imposed from without. Ezekiel likewise anticipates an altered inner life: 'A new heart also will I give you, and a new spirit will I put within you: and I will take away the stony heart out of your flesh, and I will give you a heart of flesh'. The heart will be naturally inclined to follow the divine ordinances, and people will be conscience stricken when they recall their past transgressions.[17]

The Hebrew Bible contains some graphic descriptions of the impact of conscience, particularly in the penitential psalms, but before the 'coming days' Torah is the one trustworthy source of moral discernment, and one cannot rely upon innate awareness to differentiate good and evil. As Professor Urbach points out, Jews first encounter God as the source of external authority.[18] Commandment or '*Mitzva*' remains a keystone of the Jewish vocabulary and the language of biblical revelation. But the absence of conscience is not a necessary consequence of God possessing sole authority, for the ultimate vision is that Torah will fuse with natural inclination and the heart will be at one with the divine will. Submission to external authority is not the ideal state for human beings, but the promptings of the heart are fragile and unfaithful by comparison with the clarity of revealed truth.

The Torah brings the erring heart within the prospective control of the faithful. Twice does the author of Proverbs exhort his readers to inscribe its teaching upon their own hearts: 'Let not mercy and truth forsake thee: bind them about thy neck; write them upon the table of thine heart[19] ... Keep my commandments, and live, and my law as the apple of thine eye. Bind them upon thy fingers, write them upon the table of thine heart.'[20] The wisdom of Torah will create an intrinsically spiritual personality: 'If thou seekest her as silver, and searchest for her as for hid treasures, then shalt thou understand the fear of the Lord and find the knowledge of God ... Then shalt thou understand righteousness, and judgment, and equity; – yea every good path. When wisdom entereth into thine heart, and knowledge is pleasant unto thy soul ...'[21] The reader is given the possibility of creating anew the powers of conscience, for the erring heart will be restored and corrected. 'Trust in the Lord with all thine heart; and lean not unto thine own understanding. In all thy ways acknowledge him, and he shall direct thy paths.'[22]

Rabbinic Judaism

Rabbinic Judaism speaks of the inner life in terms of two drives or inclinations, one of which is good and the second evil. They are known as the *Yetzer Hatov* (good inclination) and the *Yetzer Hara* (evil inclination). The word *Yetzer* is used several times in the Bible, notably in the Genesis material from the Noah story cited above. The phrase concerning the nature of man's heart being evil from his youth[23] translates the Hebrew: *'Yetzer lev ha'adam ra mineurav'*. *Yetzer lev* refers to the imaginings or inclination of the heart.[24] The word *Yetzer* literally means 'form' and is related to one of the verbs meaning to create.

While these concepts are derived from biblical sources, certain distinctions are deserving of note. Whereas the Bible uses the term 'heart' to describe an undifferentiated inner life, the rabbis have abstracted and formalised two distinct drives. Also, there is a far greater emphasis on the *Yetzer Hara* than its good counterpart.[25]

Unlike in the Bible the different inclinations are personified, and people enter into dialogue with them. (It is possible that this was a device used in popular preaching but it also reflects an introspective engagement that is novel.) The power of the *Yetzer Hara* is formidable, although it does not overwhelm human freedom. It is dynamic and develops in strength as we grow older. According to one interpretation the *Yetzer Hara* is innate, whereas the *Yetzer Hatov* develops later.

A most interesting feature of the *Yetzer Hara* is that some sources identified it with the essential drives of human life: 'It was very good' (Gen. 1. 31). R. Nachman said in the name of Samuel: 'That is the evil inclination. But is the evil inclination very good? Yes, for if it were not for the evil inclination, man would not build a house, or take a wife, or beget a child, or engage in business ...'[26] Other sources emphasize that we are obliged to love God with both inclinations, the evil as well as the good. According to this view, the evil inclination is not only a force that directs us to commit wrong acts, it is the very energy that infuses physical and biological existence, and can be directed to good purpose. Only when the drives become dominant forces and their objects are seen as ends in their own right, does the inclination take on an evil character.

Can the good inclination be identified with conscience? A clear description is given by the medieval commentator R. David Kimche, who maintains that while the evil inclination is innate, the good inclination is to be identified with the development of intellectual understanding. People are born with the capacity for understanding, but it only develops as we mature. Until then the *Yetzer Hara* is in sole possession. Whereas the *Yetzer Hara* describes innate and developing psychological forces, the good inclination is wholly different. As we understand more, so we are aware of the character of our drives and can properly harness and direct them. While intellectual ability is innate, disciplined understanding is acquired only in the course of study, so permitting rational analysis and control of inner dispositions. This is wholly different from conscience.[27]

Once again the antidote to evil tendencies is located externally: traditional people do not find refuge in conscience, rather they turn to the Torah for succour: 'In the school of R. Ishmael it was taught: if this abomination [the *Yetzer Hara*] meets you, drag it to the House of Study [where the Torah is learned]; if it is hard as stone it will be crushed; if it is hard as iron, it will be broken in pieces'. Another source has God saying to the Israelites: 'As long as you occupy yourselves with the Torah, the *Yetzer* will not rule over you. But if you do not occupy yourselves with the Torah, then you will be delivered into the power of the *Yetzer* and all its activity will be against you.'[28]

That the *Yetzer* is not essentially evil and that human beings are given the capacity to refashion it as an instrument for the love of God, are powerful insights into the creative capacity with which we have been endowed, inspiring the tradition to fashion character so that certain moral qualities are internalized. The ultimate attainment will be a conscience, engaged by family, community and the wider world.

The moral qualities to be internalized are clarified by the doctrine of the Imitation of God. R. Hama bar Hanina derived the principle from the verse in Deuteronomy (13:4). 'After the Lord your God you shall walk', and comments 'How can man walk after God? Is he not a consuming fire? What is meant is that man ought to walk after the Divine attributes. Just as the Lord clothes the naked, attends the sick, comforts the mourner and buries the dead, do thou likewise.'[29]

A second source emphasises qualities rather than specific actions:

> Just as the ways of heaven are graciousness and the bestowal of undeserved favours both to those who know Him and to those who do not know Him, so do you bestow kindness upon one another. Just as the ways of heaven are patient with the wicked ... so do you be patient with one another ... but do not be patient [indifferent] in the presence of each other's troubles. Just as the ways of heaven are an abundance of mercy and inclination towards mercy, so do you incline yourselves toward mercy rather than towards vindictiveness.[30]

Other key attributes are truthfulness and abundant lovingkindness. As one contemporary scholar puts it: 'Like God, human beings can attain Godliness, wisdom, love, friendliness, uniqueness, righteousness and holiness.'[31] When these qualities are internalized the individual will be guided by them: when people are tempted to stray in the direction of unrestrained egoism, an inner sense of godliness will be the voice of a troubled conscience.

The Maimonidean conscience

Some of the trends we have observed are further developed in the writings of the great philosopher and jurist Moses Maimonides. Maimonides lived in the twelfth century, and he has exerted an abiding influence on Jewish thought. An outstanding modern commentator, Professor Marvin Fox, contrasts Maimonides' view of moral obligation with natural law theory. The existence of natural law gives great weight to the role of conscience but Moses Maimonides appears to have rejected the theory, preferring to emphasize the unique veracity of divine revelation.[32]

Natural law achieved its clearest form in Stoic philosophy. Cicero describes it as follows:

> True law is right reason in agreement with nature; it is of universal application, unchanging and everlasting; it summons to duty by its commandments and averts from wrongdoing by its prohibitions ... we cannot be freed from its obligations by senate or people, and *we need not look outside ourselves for an expounder or interpreter of it* ... one eternal, unchangeable law will be valid for all nations and all times.[33]

The existence of an eternal law to be found within ourselves is clearly at odds with the notion that the revealed commandments of God are the only source of knowledge of good and evil. Furthermore, the Hebrew Bible has no word for nature: the world and humanity are created by God, sustained by him and subject to his will: only this makes them intelligible. Marvin Fox strongly disputes the view that some rabbinic passages indicate a pre-existent natural law. He further claims that medieval Jewish philosophers resisted the notion, only referring to it in a small number of instances.[34]

The Maimonidean material is particularly cogent. The

Talmud lists seven moral commandments that are universally binding. Maimonides clarifies the established rabbinic ruling that gentiles observing these precepts are the 'righteous of the nations of the world' who are guaranteed a position 'in the world to come'. The seven commandments might be taken as a basis for a Jewish theory of natural law, but Maimonides' language clearly and deliberately excludes such a possibility:

> Any person who accepts the seven commandments and is meticulous in observing them is thereby one of the righteous of the nations of the world and has a portion in the world to come. *This is only the case if he accepts them and observes them because God commanded them in the Torah, and taught us through our teacher Moses, that the children of Noah* [a term for gentiles] *had been commanded to observe them even before the Torah was given.* But if he observes them because of his own conclusions based on reason ... then he is not one of the righteous of the nations ... nor is he one of their wise men.[35]

This quite extraordinary text goes significantly beyond its classical sources, in excluding those who observe the commandments on the basis of reason alone. For our purposes such an exclusion would apply equally to those who are moral on grounds of conscience rather than religious obligation. While a famously counter-intuitive rabbinic dictum maintains that a person who acts in fulfilment of a divine command is greater than one who does similarly of his own volition, Maimonides' exclusion seems to go far further and Fox argues that it is consistent with his frequent denial that moral rules are either based on reason or capable of demonstration. The ultimate logic of a belief in revealed truth is that we no longer need (human) 'laws and *nomoi*[36]; for divine laws govern human conduct.'[37] Furthermore, it can be shown intrinsically that revealed legislation is superior to the positive laws of civil society because it is concerned with achieving human perfection, both materially and spiritually, rather than being confined to the restraint of social evils.

Maimonides' view of conscience would be equally coloured by his description of the fallen state of humanity, consequent upon the opening narrative of the Bible. Prior to the fall the first human beings possessed intellect uncompromised by the desires of the imagination or the pleasures of the senses. Pure apprehension knew only truth and falsehood and those who possessed it lived a quasi-angelic existence. The first human beings had no faculty other than a clear intellectual discernment, but they were deprived of this clarity as a consequence of their transgression. Innate 'intellectual apprehension' was no more and judgement was clouded by the promptings of an errant heart. Pure truth was known only to God and revelation was therefore the only possibility of restoring primeval spiritual attainment.[38]

Maimonides *was* concerned about the inner quality of the moral life. His code of Jewish law provides a systematic analysis of the different dispositions of character which combines Aristotle's notion of the middle way with the traditional doctrine of *Imitatio Dei*. The Aristotelian approach is frequently modified in favour of rabbinic teaching.[39]

Furthermore, Maimonides concludes his *Guide for the Perplexed* with a discussion of Jeremiah 9.23. The biblical prophet advises his reader not to seek the glories of power, wealth or intellectual attainment: 'But let him that glorieth glory in this, that he understandeth and knoweth me, that I am the Lord who exercises mercy, justice and righteousness in the earth, for in these things I delight, saith the Lord.'[40]

Maimonides notes that his proof text does not conclude with the intellectual apprehension of God: rather it insists that the divine qualities of loving kindness, judgement and righteousness must be known and imitated. The contemplation of God must ultimately transform the personality, endowing it with the social virtues that characterize God's providential guidance of the world.

Maimonides' students, particularly if they have achieved the love of God described so passionately elsewhere in his teaching,[41] will be moved to reflect the divine qualities in every fibre of their being. For Maimonides, ultimate spiritual attainment is a religious idealism wherein right acting is inspired by an impassioned apprehension of the divine will. This is the Maimonidean conscience.

Conscience and authority

For Maimonides, spiritual attainment presupposes the discipline of traditional law, or *halakha*. The commandments are for the discipline and guidance of the faculties of the soul. For example, biblical law forbids revenge and demands that we assist one who hates us when his ox or ass has fallen by the way. These laws weaken the force of wrath or anger. Obligation to restore a lost article to its owner removes the disposition of avarice. Modesty is inculcated by obligation to honour parents and the aged, but commandments to rebuke wrongdoers and boldly contradict the false prophet ensure that the observant Jew will not be timorous when confronted by evil.[42] Similarly, commandments concerned with prayer and religious observance recall the errant spirit and focus concentration upon divine service.

It is the discipline of law that enables individuals gradually to internalize awe and reverence in the presence of God: actions and their repetition are the necessary training for ultimate spiritual attainment. Awe and reverence blend with passionate devotion when men and women contemplate the knowledge of the divine that the tradition imparts, meditating upon the transcendent unity of God.[43] The discipline of *halakha* creates the inner force of personal conscience.

But classical Judaism is a legal tradition, founded ultimately upon revealed truth and elaborated by the rabbis of Israel with divine sanction. For Maimonides, *halakha* differs from secular law in both its transcendent source and its ultimate spiritual purpose. In the Maimonidean conscience we indeed hear echoes of the powerful renunciations of the biblical prophets when they were confronted by religious and social evil. But what of the independent mind? Can there be a clash between revealed truth and individual conscience? Are the ideals and values of the tradition ever in conflict with its legal structure?

The biblical echoes are ambivalent. Abraham challenged God's proposed destruction of Sodom on the grounds that it would be in conflict with divine justice if the righteous perished with the wicked.[44] (The rabbis are critical of Noah for not mounting a similar response when he was told about the coming catastrophe of the flood.)[45] But Abraham and Isaac did not dispute the *Akeda* – the binding of Isaac prior to what appeared to be his impending sacrificial death on Mount Moriah.[46] Moses challenges God with remarkable boldness about the intensified suffering of the oppressed Israelites in Egypt,[47] and psalmists and prophets contend with God in similar circumstances centuries later.[48] Job successfully challenges the misplaced theodicies of his comforters, but ultimately admits that the divine will cannot be fathomed by mortal beings.[49]

Later responses to individual conscience are complex and can evoke considerable systemic tensions. The material is technical and full examination is beyond the scope of the present essay, so analysis will be confined to certain salient points.

Biblical writ concerning religious rulings emphasizes the authority of judges, who are bound by the decisions of the majority of their colleagues. Individuals are not encouraged to follow their own interpretation or to be guided by conscience alone.

R. Aaron Halevi, author of a classic medieval text book on the commandments, explains how traditional society perceived and justified these scriptural injunctions. The key argument is that if every individual was given decisive power to interpret the tradition according to his reason, division and conflict would inevitably ensue. Structural discipline is essential if order is to be maintained and social chaos avoided.

R. Aaron Halevi also focuses upon the wisdom and scholarship of those who attain the highest religious office. If ordinary people accept their guidance and study their works with effort and devotion then truth will be attained. Most of us are not blessed with great intellectual capacity and if we follow the line of our own thoughts, little will be achieved. (R. Halevi's argument presupposes the great respect accorded to the rabbinic scholar, who was seen as both sage and religious exemplar.)[50]

A further moot point is that for R. Aaron Halevi we must abide by rabbinic guidance even if it appears contrary to reason. Even if an occasional decision is mistaken, it is better to bear with it rather than risk the destructive consequences of dissent. Error will be rare: most decisions will be reliable. But if the religious structure is subverted the consequences will be destructive for faith and the good order of society.

A second medieval commentator and major rabbinic author-ity, Moses Nachmanides, concurs that rulings must be followed even if they are apparently in error, 'For God's spirit is upon the "ministers of his sanctuary" (Ezek. 45.4)', and 'He does not abandon his pious ones; they are preserved forever (Ps. 37.28) from error and stumbling'.[51]

These views have been influential in traditional circles down the generations. A twentieth century rabbinic leader, R. Elijah Dessler, movingly recalled being present at the meet-ings of leading eastern European rabbinic figures in the years before the Holocaust: 'Whoever was present at their meetings could have no doubt that he could see the *Shechina* [divine presence] resting on the work of their hands for the Holy Spirit[52] was present in their assemblies ... Our rabbis have told us to listen to the words of the sages, even if they tell us that right is left, and not to say, heaven forbid, that they have erred ...'

A second twentieth-century scholar, R. Aryeh Frommer, echoed these sentiments, emphasizing the importance of submitting to the views of great religious authorities 'even in a case where we feel the truth is with us'. Remarkably, he cites the biblical example of the Binding of Isaac as a primary source: Isaac submitted to the authority of Abraham, despite his own reservations, and he endowed his descendants with a similar capacity in all of their generations.[53]

The endowment of the sages with transcendent authority is rooted in a rabbinic reading of Deut 17.11. The verse, speak-ing of the highest court, states: 'Thou shalt not turn aside from the sentence which they shall declare unto thee, to the right hand nor to the left'. The *Sifre*, a very early rabbinic reading, states: 'Even if it appears to you that they are saying that right is left and left is right, listen to them'.

But a different view appears in the Jerusalem Talmud: 'One might think that if they tell you that right is left and left is right, you must listen to them. Therefore the verse tells you [the contrary] ...'[54]

The second view seems wholly to contradict the first, and

it has been given substantial support by both the Talmud and Maimonides' code. For the second view, there is no obligation to follow a ruling that appears to be plainly in error, and, apparently, every reason to dissent from it. Rabbinic authority is rational, rather than transcendent or incontrovertible, and individual dissent can be obligatory. A minor difference in the two readings is of extraordinary consequence for Jewish law, community, rabbinate and individual conscience.

Today different orthodox Jewish communities follow different lines. Traditionalist orthodoxy is drawn to the notion of transcendent authority; modernist orthodoxy prefers the second, rational model. Lawrence Kaplan, a modern orthodox American academic, claims that this disagreement reflects a profound fissure: namely, the different relative weights they (the two communities) assign to submission, authority and self-overcoming, on the one hand, and autonomy, independence and self-expression on the other.

Kaplan correctly observes the conflict of modern consciousness with notions of traditional authority, but the contrasting responses he describes are inherent in Jewish tradition, which is the common property of both modern and traditional orthodoxy. Both share a heritage which demands independent intellectual endeavour, and modern orthodox writers tend to yearn for a creative application of the authority that they find within the tradition, rather than a more secular form of independence and self-expression. The differences are derived from elective affinities with contrasting aspects of traditional culture which coexist amidst considerable tension.

Intellectual independence

Jewish tradition combines emphasis upon authority with an extraordinary capacity to encourage intellectual creativity and independence. The tension is clearly illustrated in the application of traditional law, which is a central focus of Jewish religious life.

The rabbinic decisor will be mindful of discussion upon the matter in hand that spans the ages. He will be aware of radically divergent opinions each of which must be heard and examined. No two cases are entirely alike and complex data must be analysed in the light of principles and precedents. The moral imperatives of the tradition might well be evoked by the plight of the litigant and brought into play before a verdict is reached.

The personality of the *halakhic* decisor is memorably described by R. Abraham Maimonides (1186–1237) a distinguished jurist and saintly figure whose memory has been somewhat overshadowed by that of his pre-eminent father. He wrote as follows:

> I affirm that a judge who is guided in his decisions only by that which is written and explicit is both weak and timid, and such a course will result in the annulment of the dictum that the judge must be guided by his own understanding of the evidence before him ... the many precedents ... were not recorded in the Talmud for no purpose, but, equally they were not intended to dictate the decision in accordance with what is mentioned there. Rather they are intended to facilitate the ability of the sage, who has heard them many times, to engage in intellectual analysis [*shikkul ha-da'at*] and to render decisions appropriately.[55]

When Moses Maimonides codified the qualities expected of Judges he demanded that they combine the courage to save the oppressed from the oppressor with the humility of Moses, their greatest exemplar. They must be men of truth who pursue justice as an ingrained personal disposition, who love truth and detest violence and flee from all types of injustice. The judge personifies the Maimonidean conscience. The dispositions Maimonides codifies are not desiderata; they are essential qualifications that a candidate must be known to possess before he will be appointed.[56]

The presence or absence of these qualities drastically affects the fabric of traditional life. The Talmud records a case of a violent man, Mari bar Isak, who so intimidated prosecution witnesses that they would not testify against him. It happened that Mari's father died. A second person appeared claiming to be Mari's brother and demanded his share of the family inheritance. Mari bar Isak denied that the newcomer was his brother and the witnesses were so fearful that they refused to testify. In Jewish law, the burden of proof falls upon the claimant and he (the brother) was unable to sustain his case.[57]

The judge, R. Hisda, could abide by the law and dismiss the claimant for lack of evidence. He chose, however, to achieve justice by switching the burden of proof to the defendant. Mari would have to prove that the newcomer was *not* his brother. Mari complained that he was not being accorded due process but R. Hisda dismissed his protest out of hand.

A plain reading of the case indicates that R. Hisda departed from time-honoured convention in the interests of justice. He was intimidated neither by threat of violence nor by the authority of a well-established convention in a highly conservative environment and he was not disturbed by the prospect of compromising his reputation when his verdict became public knowledge. R. Hisda's judicial conscience impelled him to break with formal law, rescue the oppressed from the oppressor and defend his court from the encroachment of violent men. Rabbinic judges down the ages intervened with similar creativity in issues ranging from women's marital rights to the abuse of economic monopoly.

When Akaviah ben Mahallel was offered the opportunity to be the head of the Great Sanhedrin if he was prepared to withdraw his opinion in four cases where he evidently dissented from the views of his colleagues, his reply was prompt and uncompromising: 'It is better for me to be called a fool all my days than that I should become even for one hour a wicked man in the sight of God; and let not men say he withdrew his opinions for the sake of obtaining power'.[58] Furthermore, when a heavenly voice verified the dissenting opinion of Rabbi Eliezer the Great, his colleagues refused to retract their opposing conclusions. They had reached their verdict, and nothing on earth – or in heaven – was going to disturb them.[59] Tradition records that God took delight in the prowess of his children. (This reading appeals to the modern mentality. R. Aaron Halevi read the same incident as the proper triumph of a majority view over dissenting individual opinion, albeit that R. Eliezer was supported by heavenly intervention.)

Two very different readings of the nature of tradition emerge from a further Talmudic incident. When Resh Lakhish died, his colleague and teacher R. Yochanan was inconsolable. R. Eliezer Ben Pedat endeavoured to comfort R. Yochanan by studying Torah with him. Whatever R.

Yochanan taught, R. Eliezer Ben Pedat agreed that authoritative sources supported his view. R. Yochanan informed R.
Eliezer Ben Pedat that he was not like Resh Lakhish. When
Resh Lakhish learned a tradition he would raise many objections which R. Yochanan had to wrestle with before matters
became clear in the process of argument. R. Yochanan dryly
informed R. Eliezer Ben Pedat that he knew he had quoted
correctly and he wanted Eliezer's creative dissent rather than
his confirmation. He tore his garments, sobbing and crying
out: 'Where are you, Ben Lakhish ... where are you?'

R. Yochanan and Resh Lakhish were not sitting in court,
debating the finer points of a case in hand; they were studying Torah together, pursuing truth amidst a passionate debate
that is the hallmark of the Talmudic schools (*Yeshivot*) to this
day. The study of Torah is the obligation of every Jewish individual; such debate is to be found in both modern orthodoxy
and the more traditional communities. Young Jewish minds
are nurtured by the vigorous argumentation of R. Yochanan
and Resh Lakhish, whose spirit evidently triumphed over the
conservatism of Eliezer Ben Pedat.[60]

The essence of their approach is conveyed in a memoir of
Rabbi J. B. Soloveitchik, one of the greatest modern orthodox
rabbis, written by a former student, David Hartman, Hartman
recalled:

> the enormous sense of intellectual courage and daring that
> Soloveitchik would manifest in a talmudic lecture. No figure of
> authority would intimidate him, no quoting of Jewish sources
> would in any way inhibit his own piercing creative mind.
> Maimonides and Akiva, all the revered teachers of the past, were
> his colleagues as he studied the Talmud. He argued with them, he
> struggled with them. They were living people who encouraged
> him in a discussion. His own uncompromising commitment to
> intellectual honesty, his refusal to say that he understood as long
> as anything remained unclear, his ability to assert his own intel-
> lectual independence in the face of the whole tradition, this was
> Soloveitchik's own manifest experience of talmudic learning in
> the Brisk (a Lithuanian centre of talmudic learning that empha-
> sized rigorous conceptual analysis) tradition.

R. Soloveitchik explained that '*Halakhic* man' was moved
by a combination of deep piety and a passionate love of truth:

'He recognises no authority other than the authority of the intellect (obviously, in accordance with the principles of tradition). He hates intellectual compromises ...' The bracketed phrase should be noted, but R. Soloveitchik believed that the autonomy of the intellect that he had portrayed reached heights that were 'unimaginable in any other religion'.[61]

David Hartman, perceptively noted that 'since learning itself is regarded as a religious act by Orthodox Jews, such independence must spill over into the normative life that talmudic study elucidated'. R. Soloveitchik himself claimed that biblical law is not experienced by traditional Jews as something extraneous or coerced, but is felt to be the personal existential law of their own being. For R. Soloveitchik humanity is not the passive recipient of divine authority but rather a partner with God in the work of creation. The most fervent desire of *Halakhic* man is 'to behold the replenishment of the deficiency in creation, when the real world will conform to the ideal world and ... the ideal *Halakha* ... will be actualized in its midst. The dream of creation is the central idea in the *halakhic* consciousness, which is focused upon the importance of man as a partner of the Almighty in the act of creation, man as a creator of worlds.'[62]

Conscience, tension and conflict

Biblical ideals are the ultimate aspirations of *halakha* and can sometimes transcend the formal letter of law. When Rabbah bar Bar Hannah employed porters who broke a barrel of wine inadvertently, he took their garments from them as compensation and refused to pay their wages. Both measures were legally warranted for he had suffered a considerable loss as a result of their negligence. The porters appealed against him successfully. Rabbah bar Bar Hannah had to return the garments and pay the porters for their day's work. They were poor people who had worked all day and were hungry. The judge maintained that the biblical ideals of righteous social conduct set aside the formalities of the law of negligence.[63]

When Moses Maimonides codified the scriptural law that it was permitted to work a heathen slave 'with rigour', he simultaneously abrogated it, for while such was 'the rule', it was consonant neither with the quality of piety nor the way of wisdom, both of which demanded mercy and the pursuit of justice. The student of the law would learn to disparage idolatry, but practical social conduct must be guided by larger principle.[64]

Nevertheless, for the modern Jewish conscience there are frequently tensions and inner conflicts with the traditional sources. Marvin Fox lists well-known biblical examples and comments bluntly that some scriptural commands 'seem to be an offence to our ideas of common morality, and even more, to the spirit of His [God's] own teaching'. Referring to the obligation to wage war relentlessly on the inhabitants of Canaan he admits that the destruction was not 'wanton' and the Canaanite cults were idolatrous and irreconcilable with the service of one God. Nevertheless, 'for many modern readers these passages generate great discomfort, agony and even revulsion, because they seem to be so contrary to what we usually understand by Jewish morality.'[65]

Fox argues that:

> For the traditionalist God is the source of all notions of right and wrong. In some ultimate sense what is required of us must be truly good, for a God whose commandments are evil would not be truly God. This certainly makes it permissible to question him in cases of seeming injustice but never to reject him or his commandments.

Even Job, who comes closer than anyone to a direct denial of God's justice is finally reconciled once he confronts the divine majesty. He still has no answers, but his faith in God's righteousness is restored. He spoke without understanding of things beyond him, which he did not know. Without the divine moral standard, there is no standard at all.

Traditionalists take refuge in the divine wisdom, and emphasise that the thrust of biblical tradition as a whole is peaceful rather than bellicose. The conquest of Canaan was not seen as a precedent nor did it govern the development of Jewish culture. David, a great military figure, was forbidden to build the Temple because he had shed much blood in his battles.[66] The ultimate Judaic vision is one of universal peace, but the founding narratives instil in the reader an awareness that culture can sink to very great depths and even the righteous have sometimes to give battle despite all of their contrary inclinations. Paradoxically the reader of Joshua and Judges is made equally aware of the tragic impact of conflict upon the Israelites whose moral sensitivities are gradually corroded as the narratives develop, recovering only with the coming of the age of Samuel.

A second source of conflict for the modern Jewish conscience lies within the contemporary application of some aspects of *Halakha*.[67] Traditional societies see themselves as culturally embattled amidst the powerful trends of contemporary life. At odds with the radical adaptations made by Progressive and Conservative Jews their instincts are defensive rather than creative. In a most influential centre of Jewish culture, the United States, less than 10 per cent of Jews remain orthodox, and they are not inclined to pursue radical innovations that might further corrode traditional observance. Jewish sources contain many diverse strands and radicalism is balanced by a highly conservative respect for the customs, practices and decisions of revered figures in previous generations. Furthermore, in contemporary orthodoxy, religious authorities often live in traditional milieux that are very different from the modern culture that has created conflict and tension for many observant men and women.

Key problems revolve about the status of women. For example, in recent years much attention has been paid to a modern variant of the age old difficulty presented by the plight of *agunah*, the woman unable to remarry in the absence of a formal bill of divorce from her husband, or acceptable evidence that he had died. Civil facilities have enabled husbands to divorce their wives without going through the requisite religious procedure. In Jewish law, such women are still considered married, and any further union would be regarded as adulterous. Rabbinic authorities have been reluctant to sanction annulment proceedings or to make use of preventative remedies in marriage contracts that are available to them, albeit rarely used down the ages. No one disputes that the law can be abused by persons who are acting in their own advantage, and that the wife (or, rarely the husband) suffers unwarranted trauma. But the *Halakhic* conscience has been inhibited by factors described above, despite learned submission from scholarly rabbis of whom Eliezer Berkovits is the most notable. (In Great Britain Lord Jakobovits has made a major contribution to solving the problem via the new civil divorce legislation, which should forestall further abuses.)

The *agunah* case is worthy of note within the context of the role of conscience in traditional Jewish society. It is a classical example of Maimonides' difficult statement that no system of law can deal satisfactorily with every conceivable circumstance: 'The law pays no attention to what happens rarely or to the damage occurring to the unique individual because of … the legal character of governance'.[68] The law by definition must be concerned with the general utility and damages to individuals may necessarily occur.

The stability of marriage is a vital social concern and adultery is a grave transgression. To permit a woman to remarry when her wedded husband might still be alive is very difficult indeed. (Men can find themselves in similar situations, but there are rarely used remedies. The Bible, unlike later Jewish practice, permits polygamy while strictly proscribing polyandry, the female equivalent. The remedies reflect this asymmetry.) It runs the risk of creating an adulterous union. The children of such a union will be deemed illegitimate with considerable consequence for their future marital status.

Adultery is an absolute proscription. Classically, if a man has relations with a married woman, both can, in theory, suffer the ultimate penalty. In practice, the demands made by the laws of evidence would make that improbable, but the gravity of the offence remains. The sanctity of the marital relationship and the laws that protect it can create suffering for a woman who cannot prove that her husband is deceased. The woman is Maimonides' unique individual, confronted by the demands of general utility, and the law cannot help her, for it cannot sanction what might well be an adulterous relationship.

The remedy of retrospective annulment of the marriage was never used in *agunah* cases. The assumption was that the husband was still alive, and his marriage could not be annulled without evidence of his consent. What Eliezer Berkovits has called the *Halakhic* conscience was not stilled and Rabbis, basing themselves on the assumption that a woman would make every possible enquiry before remarriage, admitted evidence in her favour that would have been deemed unacceptable in any other context. Rabbis have wrestled with these problems down the ages, particularly in times of war, when verification of death can be very difficult, but many cases have remained unresolved.

Holy writ guarantees the sanctity of the marital bond. The *Halakhist's* conscience hears both the needs of the beleaguered *agunah* and the feelings of the husband who is presumed alive in the absence of evidence to the contrary. He seeks an optimum solution, but in the nature of the cases this is not always achievable. Conscience is drawn in conflicting directions simultaneously: obligation to the divine will regarding adultery, and an equally mandated compassion for husband and wife, create a dilemma that cannot be reconciled within the traditional framework.

Agunah and other problems of personal relationships are further complicated by the subtle changes in perception of familial structures which were taken for granted in the age of classical Judaism. Levirate marriage, the obligation of a man to marry the widow of a brother who died childless and to perpetuate his name by fathering children, assumed a view of the family and its loyalties that no longer pertains. Even the *agunah* problem is rooted in an absolute sense of the marital bond that is rapidly passing away. Laws rooted in socio-cultural contexts that the tradition took for granted are rendered rootless and the moral universe that inspired them is no more. Even in most traditional societies, levirate marriage was abandoned long ago, but a ceremonial breaking of the putative bond is still practised in orthodoxy. The conscience of traditional people is profoundly affected by cultural changes so long term as to be almost imperceptible.

Progressive and Liberal Jews have abandoned the remnant of levirate marriage and arrange divorce proceedings if they are troubled by *agunah*, coming down squarely in favour of the beleaguered wife, so the problem effectively disappears. Orthodoxy differs, not in matters of conscience, but in its belief that the absolutes of the divine fiat are timeless and remain sacred for ever. Orthodox rabbis are certainly moved by their conscience to alleviate the plight of *agunah*, but their frame of reference is different, and they are guided by traditional parameters. (After Israel's 1973 war the rabbinate headed by R. Ovadiah Yosef addressed and solved about one thousand cases of *agunot*, whose husbands never returned from battle.)

Judaism knows of different notions of conscience. Joseph's hesitation, and the pounding heart of King David, reflect the power of a traditional culture to evoke guilt and remorse. But the dominant image of the Judaic conscience is a product of personal endeavour to restore the erring heart to its primeval affinity with the ideals of righteousness, justice, compassion and truth. These are the qualities of divine action; in their pursuit, women and men rekindle within themselves the holiness of their creator.

The Maimonidean judge does not act righteously because he is obligated to do so, he is moved by those ideals that he has been commanded to instil within himself by his own disciplined endeavour. The great qualities of biblical idealism are fused with the heights of spiritual attainment: the two are neither separate nor distinct. We are at one with God when we replicate within ourselves the ideals manifested by the biblical prophets. A truly profound love of God creates an impassioned desire for that divine idealism which is the prophetic response to the world. In its pursuit, women and men become holy, as the Lord their God is holy.

Conscience is born in a deliberate and disciplined act of personal creation. When it encounters an apparently countervailing force of traditional authority or the innate restrictions of the discipline of law, diverse responses are evoked.

Legal formality can be set aside in order to safeguard justice, as when a violent man seeks to intimidate the plaintiff's witnesses, and the judge intervenes creatively on the plaintiff's behalf. Employers can be asked to sacrifice a legal right in the interest of compassion for poor labourers and pay their wages even when they have suffered loss due to their labourers' negligence. Traditional law, which has religious force, is set aside in favour of ultimate idealism, and the judge is guided by conscience rather than purely formal consideration.

But there are boundaries. The prospect of creating an adulterous relationship and drastically infringing divine writ guarantees formalistic consideration in cases of *agunah*, leaving women whose husbands have disappeared unable to enter into a new relationship. The woman suffers through no fault of her own; if evidence of her husband's death is inadequate, little can be done. Conscience is directed into conflicting areas, and the authority of divine commandment is decisive. The progressive Jewish conscience prioritizes the plight of the woman, but the dilemma is ultimately the same.

Traditional Jewish societies encompass radically different responses to authority which cut across the promptings of the heart. The binding of Isaac, the *Akeda*, is a powerful symbol of self-abnegation in the presence of the divine. Reverence for religious authority nullifies intellectual reservation and demands a suspension of conscience reminiscent of Abraham on Mount Moriah. Self-abnegation in the spirit of *Akeda* is the beginning of true devotion.

Over and against this stands the equally compelling image of Abraham at Sodom, challenging the judge of all the earth to do justice. Humble but uninhibited, Abraham defends those who will be wronged by divine fiat. In the awesome presence of God, this too is an act of self-sacrifice. It is the world of Resh Lakhish in the presence of R. Yochanan, and Rabbi J. B. Soloveitchik teaching his students Torah in twentieth-century America.

Both images coexist, creating conflict and powerful tensions within a bipolar religious life. The *Akeda* is indeed the beginning of true devotion, but it is achieved in the presence of a God who demands loving kindness, righteousness and judgement on earth. Self-sacrifice is not nullity: it is an act of transformation wherein the faithful will reflect those ideals that are the ways of the divine, rather than the promptings of an errant heart. It is the creation of conscience, which for Moses Maimonides was the height of the spiritual life.

Notes

1.   Gen. 39.8.

2. Genesis Rabba 87.7.
3. Talmud Bavli, Sotah 36b.
4. 1 Sam. 25.36–37.
5. J. B. Soloveitchik, *Al Hateshuvah* (Jerusalem, 1989), p. 28.
6. 1 Sam. 24.5–6.
7. 2 Sam. 24.10.
8. Gen. 8.21.
9. Num. 15.39.
10. Deut. 11.16.
11. Eccles. 7.29.
12. 1 Chron. 28.9.
13. 1 Chron. 29.18–19.
14. 1 Kings 3.9.
15. 1 Kings 3.12.
16. Jer. 31.31–33.
17. Ezek. 11.19; 36.26.
18. Urbach, *Chazal, Pirkei Emunot VeDest* (Jerusalem, 1969), p. 279.
19. Prov. 3.3.
20. Prov. 7.2–3.
21. Prov. 2.4–5, 9–10.
22. Prov. 3.5–6.
23. Gen. 8.21.
24. Gen. 8.21.
25. For rabbinic sources see G. G. Montefiore and H. Loewe (eds), *A Rabbinic Anthology* (London, 1938), pp. 295–314.
26. For R. Nachman's comment on Gen. 1.31 see Genesis Rabba 9.7; ibid., p. 305.
    The rabbinic material dates approximately from the first to the fifth century; see the lengthy discussion at the end of the *Anthology* (see note 25 above) for more detail.
27. Commentary on Gen. 8.21; *Torat Chaim* (Jerusalem, 1986), p. 121.
28. T. B. Kiddushin, p. 30b.
29. For R. Hama bar Hanina see T. B. Sotah, 14a.
30. The second source is from Midrash Tanhuman Vayishlach 10.
31. D. S. Shapiro, 'The Doctrine of the Image of God and *Imitatio Dei* in M. Kellner (ed.), *Contemporary Jewish Ethics* (New York, 1978), pp. 127–151.
32. M. Fox, *Interpreting Maimonides* (University of Chicago Press, Chicago, 1990), pp. 124–151.
33. Cicero, *De Re Publica* III. xxii. 33.
34. For a contrary view, see L. Jacobs, 'The Relationship between

Religion and Ethics in Jewish Thought' in M. M. Kellner, op. cit., pp. 41–57.

35. Maimonides, *Hilchot Melakhim*, 8.11, cited in Fox, op. cit., p. 132. The Noachide commandments prohibit idolatry, blasphemy, murder, adultery, robbery and eating the limb of a living animal. Also, there is an obligation to establish courts of justice.
36. *nomoi* – rational conventions, laws derived by philosophers.
37. Maimonides, *Treatise on Logic*, ed. Efros, 64, cited in Fox, op. cit., p. 134. The view that one who is commanded is greater than one who acts of his own volition is stated in T. B. Kiddushin 31a.
38. Maimonides, *Guide for the Perplexed* II, id. p. 280, cited in Fox, op. cit., p. 188.
39. For an excellent selection of Maimonidean material see I. Twersky, *A Maimonides Reader* (Behrman House, New York, 1972). For moral dispositions, see Twersky, pp. 61–63.
40. For the last chapter of *Guide* see pp. 357–358.
41. For the passionate love of God, see the last chapter of *Hilchot Teshuva* (The Laws of Penitence) pp. 84–85.
42. Maimonides, *Eight Chapters*, chapter 4: Twersky, op. cit., p. 373.
43. Maimonides, *Guide for the Perplexed*, chapter 21: Twersky, op. cit., pp. 345, 350.
44. Gen. 18.23.
45. The criticism of Noah by comparison with Abraham is to be found in the mystical work, the Zohar, commenting on Genesis. See D. C. Matt (tr.) *Zohar, The Book of Enlightenment* (SPCK, 1983), pp. 57–59, for a translation.
46. The *Akeda* story is in Genesis 22.
47. Moses' challenge to God is at Exod. 5.22–23.
48. Psalm 44 is a well-known psalm of protest.
49. Job 42.1–6.
50. *Sefer Hachinuch* (Eshkol, Jerusalem, n.d.), pp. 299–302.
51. Nachmanides on Deut. 17.11. For a translation and further material on this matter I am indebted to L. Kaplan. 'Daas Torah: A Modern Conception of Rabbinic Authority' in M. S. Sokol (ed.), *Rabbinic Authority and Personal Autonomy* (Jason Aronson, 1992), pp. 1–60.
52. Of course, no trinitarian understanding of God is intended here.
53. Cited in Kaplan, op. cit., pp. 16, 43–44.
54. Jerusalem and Babylonian Talmuds. Horayot 2b. Maimonides, *Hikhot Shegagot* 13.5, cited in Kaplan, op. cit., p. 29.

55. *Responsa of Rabbi Abraham, Son of the Rambam* (Jerusalem, 1937), pp. 147–148, cited in J. Roth, *The Halakhic Process, A Systemic Analysis* (Jewish Theological Seminary of America, 1986), p. 86.
56. Maimonides, *Hilkhot Sanhedrin* 2.7. Twersky, op. cit., pp. 192–193. Maimonides is more demanding than his source in Deuteronomy Rabba 1.10. The material is cited in Roth, op. cit., p. 145.
57. The case is to be found in the Babylonian Talmud. Bava Mezia 39b and Ketubot 17b. For a full discussion of the related issues, see A. Kirschenbaum, *Equity in Jewish Law* (2 vols. Ktav, Yeshiva University Press, New York, 1991).
58. For Akaviah ben Mahallel, see T. B. Eduyot, 5.6–7.
59. For R. Eliezer's dispute, see T. B. Bava Mezia 59b.
60. Bava Mezia 84a.
61. D. Hartman, *A Living Covenant* (Free Press, 1985), p. 69.
62. J. B. Soloveitchik, *Halakhic Man* (Jewish Publication Society, Philadelphia, 1983), p. 99.
63. T. B. Bava Mezia 83a. For an extended discussion see Kirschenbaum, op. cit., vol. 2, p. 121.
64. Maimonides, *Avadim* 9.8, trans. in Twersky, op. cit., p. 177.
65. M. Fox, 'Maimonides' Views on the Relations of Law and Morality', in Fox, op. cit., pp. 199–226.
66. 1 Chron. 22.8.
67. This section is heavily indebted to E. Berkovits, *Not in Heaven, The Nature and Function of Halakha* (Ktav, New York, 1983). See especially pp. 32–46 on the status of women, and pp. 100–105 on marriage and divorce laws.
68. Maimonides, *Guide for the Perplexed* 3, 34, cited in Fox, op. cit., p. 209. For discussion see Kirschenbaum, op. cit. vol. 2, p. xxxii; the Maimonidean position is not as restrictive as this much-discussed statement implies.

6

Islam and Conscience

Ron Geaves

There is a vast amount of historical sources to be studied which throw light on the development of Muslim ethics. These range from *tafsir* (exegesis of the Qur'an) to more discursive philosophical commentaries on Aristotle and ethics that are derived from *kalam* (theology). In addition, there is the vast legal work of the early jurists as they formulated the *shari'a* (Islamic law) and the contrasting mystical texts of the Sufis based on their inner experience of Allah's immanence.

However, to understand the workings of conscience within Islam it is essential to emphasize the centrality of revelation. Religious morality in Islam relies heavily on the scriptural tradition of the Qur'an and Hadith. Muslims believe that the Qur'an is the final revelation of Allah to human beings and the key to understanding the Muslim view of conscience is found in its *suras*. Consequently, the focus of this chapter will be on the scriptural tradition, but it will also explore the alternative perspective of conscience as maintained by Islam's mystical tradition.

Fakhry defined Muslim ethics as a 'reasoned account of the nature and grounds of right action and decisions and the principles underlying the claim that they are morally commendable or reprehensible'.[1] It is essential to comprehend whether actions fall into these categories of morally commendable or reprehensible in order to comprehend the formation of conscience in Islam, consequently I will use Eliade's definition that conscience is 'the faculty within us that decides on the moral quality of our thoughts, words and acts. It makes us conscious of the worth of our deeds and gives rise to pleasurable feelings if they are good and to painful ones if they are evil'.[2] The clue to how this faculty functions for Muslims is summed up in the following passage from the Qur'an:

> Let there arise out of you
> A band of people
> Inviting to all that is good,
> Enjoining what is right,
> And forbidding what is wrong:
> They are the ones
> To attain felicity.[3]

The above passage indicates that those who follow the good and prevent others from wrong-doing will be rewarded in this world and in the next. The following verse speaks of the fate of those who disobey this injunction who are sentenced to a 'dreadful penalty'.[4] Ali comments that the rewards and punishments are not only in the next world but will be manifest in this world as success, prosperity, freedom from anxiety or alternatively failure, misery, or anguish.[5] This gives rise to the important doctrine of 'Manifest Success' in which the ideal Muslim community receives the fruits of its obedience to Allah's will in this world. These manifest rewards of obedience in themselves become the proof of divine approval.[6]

Revelation and conscience

Islam actually means surrender to the will of Allah and it is important to recognise that for the majority of Muslims the self is not the judge of right and wrong. As in the Hebrew Scriptures, God is all-seeing and knows our entire being. Allah is the sole arbitrator of commendable or reprehensible actions. The Qur'an states:

> Of the good that they do,
> Nothing will be rejected
> Of them; for God knoweth well
> Those that do right.[7]

Cicero's description of the 'bite of conscience' appearing as an internal moral authority seated within the individual is alien to the Islamic concept of revelation.[8] The manifestations of conscience could not operate correctly without the intervention of the divine in human affairs. Conscience cannot be left to the arbitrary human interpretation of moral behaviour. Neither can it be assumed that the inner workings of conscience in themselves can be trusted to distinguish the good. Revelation ensures that correct action is not left to the vagaries of social upbringing or cultural norms which will vary from society to society. The Muslim belief in final judgement which results in either the reward of paradise or punishment in hell is an absolute. It is too important for a merciful God to leave it to the subjectivity of human understanding. The issue of how humanity knows what is right or wrong becomes prominent in Islam. Allah would not judge human beings without first giving them guidance. Margoulieth points out that private judgement is therefore negated and neither the Qur'an nor the Prophet emphasize instinctive notions of right and wrong.[9]

The imperative mood in Islam

The notion of hell is an important determinant in the workings of conscience since it becomes internalized as a voice which warns against wrongdoing or sin. Lodge notes that in the 1960s the concept of hell and eternal damnation disappeared for the majority of Christians in Britain.[10] This would have had an impact on the liberal or permissive morality of the era. In 1966, the Archbishop of Canterbury confirmed the view that Christian morality was not about obedience to commandments but about applying moral principles to each unique situation that arose in life. The underlying principle was love,[11] and conscience became a personal issue formed by individual understanding rather than a creation of doctrinal obedience. In interviews with Muslim informants, I have been struck by their strong belief in paradise and hell. On many occasions Muslim friends and associates have urged me to convert to Islam as they fear for my fate on the Day of

Judgement. For all Muslims this polarity of destination is reflected in the six core beliefs which are as follows:

1. the oneness of Allah
2. the omniscience of Allah
3. belief in angels
4. scriptural revelation
5. prophethood
6. reward or punishment in the life after death decided at the Day of Judgement.

These core beliefs clearly established an imperative rather than interpretative framework in which human beings could live under the sovereignty of God and in accordance with his will. The final prophethood of Muhammad is the means for the last and complete revelation of God's will. The Day of Judgement will ensure that the obedient and the disobedient will receive their just rewards. The Qur'an indicates that recording angels note every person's intentions and deeds in preparation for the final judgement.[12] Traditionally Muslims believe that there are two pairs of angels involved in the task of recording for judgement. The first pair accompany human beings throughout their life. The angel on the right-hand side of the person records all good intentions and actions, whereas the angel on the left only records actual wrongdoing.[13] Bad intentions which are not translated into action are not counted against the believer at the Day of Judgement. The Qur'an confirms the presence of these angels.

> Behold, two guardian angels
> Appointed to learn his doings
> Learn and note them,
> One sitting on the right
> And one on the left.[14]

The Qur'an also affirms the presence of Munkar and Nakir, the two angels that appear in the grave to provide initial judgement.[15] It is believed that these angels will eventually accompany the soul at the final Day of Judgement. These angels do not in any way lessen the supremacy of God's omniscience. However, they do indicate that the Muslim conscience must deal with an overwhelming sense of being observed by the divine. It should be noted that the intention of this supernatural presence is not concerned primarily with judgement but protection of the believer. Nothing can be hidden from God, but the presence of the angels acts as a deterrent to maintain the Muslim on the straight path.

Many of my Muslim informants stress that this focus on Allah's justice and judgement is modified by his overwhelming mercy. Bad deeds may be corrected by punishment in this life through ill-fortune or disease. A Muslim will also receive punishment in the grave while awaiting the final Day of Judgement, and then finally can be sentenced to a duration in hell. Ultimately, it is believed that the intercession of the Prophet on behalf of his community will liberate all Muslims to an eternal stay in Paradise. It is also believed that actions performed in this life which aid subsequent generations relieve the punishment for wrongdoing. Muslims who rear their children to honour the revelation of Allah will receive the reward of their children's piety. Those that propagate the faith by missionary endeavour or help in the construction of mosques will receive the fruits of their labour through the assistance that this gives to others throughout future generations. Likewise Muslims who perform a good deed such as constructing a well which will continue to provide water for future use will have their burden lightened in the grave every time the well is used. Thus God's justice and mercy extend from this life through to the final destination of paradise for all Muslims.

Early theological questions

Islam therefore gives precedence to orthopraxy over orthodoxy, but certain questions did concern early Muslim theologians attempting to understand the Qur'an. These focused on the problem of free-will faced with the absolute omniscience of Allah and the nature of right and wrong. Hourani points out that three positions were developed in the first three centuries:

1. values have an objective existence which can be known through the use of reason or by Scripture (the Mu'tazilite position).
2. values are whatever Allah commands. They can be known through the Qur'an and the tradition of the Prophet. If derived from the Qur'an they can be used to extend tradition (the Ash'arite position).
3. values are objective and can be known by the reasoning of wise people such as philosophers or mystics. However, they are provided to the masses by a prophet in the form of scriptural tradition.[16]

Al-Ash'ari's (*c.* 300/913) position, that although God is overwhelmingly dominant and supreme, human beings must have free will in respect of their obedience to the revelation, finally became orthodoxy. Al-Ash'ari followed the guidance of transmitted sources rather than the process of reasoning. He maintained that all humans were held responsible for their actions and culpable for their sins even though God is omniscient and omnipotent. He argued that God is the creator of the power to perform each action and therefore enables it to be performed, but the act itself is carried out by the human being who is responsible for the consequences.[17] On the issue of right and wrong, the Mu'tazilites supported the idea of an ontological good established by God at the moment of creation.[18] Therefore Allah was bound to follow the rules of his creation and be subject to the good. However, this idea diminished Allah's total sovereignty. Once again, the Ash'arite position eventually became the orthodox stance. Al-Ash'ari maintained that the good only attained its status because God decreed it so. The definition of good is that whatever Allah wills becomes good. This position of ethical voluntarism became the first principle of the four Muslim schools of law.[19] Al-Ash'ari's position shifted the emphasis from reason back to revelation. An ontological good may be discovered through rational means but revelation alone can make known what Allah has decided. Justice may be achieved through obedience to the divine law but God cannot be subject to these laws. The faculty of reason exists in order to aid human beings in their attempts to adhere to God's will. The

conscience will function to ensure that individuals place themselves in the appropriate relationship to Allah and his
commandments and thus maintain the required piety needed to
earn the reward of paradise. Muslims have a religious obligation to obey, and disobedience to God's commandments is
counted as sin (*al-ma'siyah*).

Conscience and law

Since it is God that wills what is good, and human beings have
no accurate inner voice to determine right or wrong action, [20]
it is essential that Muslims can bring the revelation to bear on
every activity in their lives. The revelation is the direction for
life and consequently, as Rahman points out, the conception
of law in Islam is essentially religious.[21] The *shari'a* is the
detailed application of the revelation into every area of human
existence. It is essential that the Qur'an functions as the direc-
tor of human life and it must be the original source of Islamic
law. It is inconceivable that a human being could be knowl-
edgeable in God's law, therefore knowing the difference
between good and evil, yet choose evil out of preference. Evil
is usually attributed to either ignorance or frailty and forget-
fulness. [22] Cragg points out that evil is not seen as 'some
radical evil, some deep perversity, where law, while identifying it for what it is, is powerless to correct it'.[23] Muslims who
find themselves in a position of having broken one of God's
commandments must be able to repent and seek forgiveness,
and therefore the law must be able to correct their situation by
guiding them back to the right path. Therefore there can be no
areas which are not covered by the law.

Muslims believe that obedience to the law is an achievable
goal and not an arduous task. Allah is ultimately merciful and
knows the human heart. He would not set a task that was
impossible or onerous. Obedience is within the human capacity. However, there is a problem for religions like Islam and
Judaism which are founded upon an historical revelation from
God to humanity which provides moral and ethical guidance
for all situations. The revelation is believed to be complete
and therefore applicable until the end of time. God in his

omniscience would not have omitted anything from the revelation, nor would he have left anything to chance and the human propensity for error. Consequently, the revelation must contain a comprehensive framework capable of dealing with all possible human situations. However, human societies change over time, and the process of change has increased dramatically since the advent of rapid developments in scienific knowledge and technology. It is essential that there is a means of interpreting the central revelation to discover God's will for all new situations that may not have existed at the time and place of revelation. The Muslim should not be in any doubt as to right and wrong behaviour.

In the first two centuries of Islam's history, Muslim scholars and jurists provided a comprehensive extension of the *shari'a* to try and fit every possible ethical situation. The study of law became the backbone of an Islamic education.[24] They realised that it was essential for all human conduct to be categorized as either obedience or disobedience to the divine edict and for this to be built into the legal codes of the rapidly expanding Islamic civilization. New territories entering into the realm of Islam brought with them customs that were not familiar to the Arabs. It was necessary to establish whether these were compatible with the revelation of God. The strictly legislative part of the Qur'an is actually quite small[25] and the jurists embarked on a massive creative programme to formulate the *shari'a* into a comprehensive programme to guide Muslims of all future generations. The first part of this interpretative process was to collect and assess the reliability of all the sayings and deeds of the Prophet. Muhammad (pbuh) was the Prophet of God and the vehicle for revelation. His conduct was perceived to be the perfect example of obedience to God's law in practice. This exemplary role of the Prophet was to lead eventually to the idea of his sinlessness. Thus the behaviour of the Prophet became the second authoritative source to complement the Qur'an in formulating the detailed *shari'a*. This is known as the *Sunna* of the Prophet and by the middle of the third/ninth century[26] six comprehensive collections (Hadith) of the Prophet's deeds and words had been collected and authorized and became known as the Six Genuine Ones.[27] It was imperative that the Hadith were genuine and in order to establish their veracity a Science of Hadith was developed. This process was founded on the biographies of the transmitters of the multitudinous reports of the Prophet's deeds and sayings. Each Hadith is given a chain of transmission (*isnad*) which traces the origin back to a Companion of the Prophet who must have heard it from the Prophet himself. The character and reliability of the chain became known as 'the Science of Justification and Impugnment'.[28] In this way Hadith were classified in four categories, as weak, truthful, unknown and completely trustworthy.

However, there were still occasions where the Qur'an and the Hadith did not provide a clear and unequivocal understanding of a particular human situation. Muhammad ibn Idris al-Shafi'i (d. 204/819) proposed that the principles of the law were to be reached in the following order:

1. The Qur'an
2. The *Sunna* of the Prophet as contained in the Hadith
3. *Ijma* or the consensus of scholars in interpreting the above two
4. *Qiyas* or the analogical reasoning from examples in the Qur'an and the *Sunna* to new situations.

Through this process by the end of the third/ ninth and the beginning of the fourth/tenth centuries both doctrine and law had been developed to such a degree that they covered the minutiae of everyday life. The scholars and jurists declared the process complete. The accumulation of legal decisions had developed into the existence of four authoritative schools of law by the third/ninth century which are still followed by Sunni Muslims throughout the world. They are as follows:

1. Shafi'i school founded by Al-Shafi'i
2. Maliki school founded by Malik ibn Anas (d. 179/795) in Medina
3. Hanbali school founded by Ahmad ibn Hanbal (d. 241/855)
4. Hanifi school founded by Abu Hanifa (d. 150/767).

These schools vary only in minor details and regard each

other as orthodox. On the whole most Muslims owe allegiance to one school or another through their geographical place of birth. [29]

As a result of this process all conduct could be judged as obedience or disobedience to the divine law. However, the Muslim conscience was externalized one step further as the law of God became enshrined into the legal structure of the various Muslim territories. Muslims living within Islamic territory where the *shari'a* law held sway not only feared the punishment of God for wrongdoing but also could find themselves receiving penalties for breaking the law of the land for the same offence. Where both earthly and divine courts punished the wrongdoer for offences against God's will, it is difficult to ascertain the degree to which individual Muslims internalized an innate sense of right and wrong in the way that conscience is usually understood in western or Christian terms. However, it needs to be remembered that the first intention of Islamic law is religious rather than legal. It exists as a system of 'dos' and 'don'ts' which express the reality of the idea of God as sovereign which lies at the very core of Islam. Ultimately the Muslim conscience will exist as the process by which humans discover and execute the divine will. The internalization of guilt and consequent repentance are part of the process of discovery.

Although the full range of human ethics has been incorporated into the *shari'a,* so that all behaviour was judged as either obedience or disobedience to divine law and also built into the legal structure, the need for personal discovery was recognized by the early scholars of Islamic jurisprudence. They realised that for a system to be genuinely all-encompassing it could not be simply limited only to acts which were forbidden and acts which were permissable by law. They developed further categories which included actions which were optional but value-laden.[30] This fivefold categorisation of actions is as follows:

i)　　*wajib*　　these are obligatory acts which Allah has commanded. Failure to perform them will be punished.

ii)　　*mandub*　　these are actions which are recommended.

		Their performance is rewarded but failure to carry them out is not punished.
iii)	*ja'iz*	these are actions to which Allah is indifferent. It is of no concern if they performed or not. Consequently, there can be no reward or punishment.
iv)	*makruh*	these are actions which are disapproved of. They are discouraged but not forbidden. Refraining from them is rewarded but performing them is not punished.
v)	*mahzur*	these are actions which are prohibited. It is forbidden to indulge in them and the participant will be punished.

Although this categorization functions to classify all possible human action within the framework of the *shari'a*, it also allows for more freedom in the process of personal discovery and consequently the development of individual conscience. Categories ii, iii, and iv, in particular, allow for individuals to search their own inner beings and make their own moral choices. Rahman points out this system came to be known as 'resoluteness and relaxation' (*'azima* and *rukhsa*). It demanded that Muslims should search in their hearts, bringing together faith, intention and will in all their religious and moral choices.[31]

Custom and law

Further flexibility was given to the Muslim by the rapid spread of Islam which incorporated a vast diversity of existing cultures into the faith. These cultures possessed existing customs which had to be negotiated when incorporating Islamic laws and mores. Moreover, the Qur'an itself acknowledged that Allah had provided previous revelations to other earlier cultures. It was apparent that these codes of behaviour differed in detail if not in principle. Shah Wali-Allah (1703–1763) of Delhi, one of the foremost scholars and mystics of the Indian subcontinent, examined the *shari'a* with the above problems uppermost in his thoughts. He separated *din* from *shari'a* and he argued that throughout human history successive revelations had been based on a primordial or archetypal ideal religion (*din*) which pre-existed the manifestations or revelations (*shari'a*). He affirmed that this primordial faith was in complete harmony with the ideal form of the human being and is suited to the inherent nature of humanity (*fitra*). The actual manifestations of the ideal are known as *milal* or religious communities guided by revelation. These may have varied slightly according to the particular historical or social circumstances of the people who received them. Religion therefore has adapted itself to the customs, previously held convictions and temperaments of the nations to whom it has been revealed. [32]

Consequently, according to Shah Wali-Allah, there are two sources of religious legislation. The first is based on the universal or natural constitution of the human being. The individuals who went against or ignored *fitra* would transgress against their own deepest nature and harm themselves. This would be felt as the voice of conscience. The second source is made up of the particular systems of law (*shari'a*) which have been revealed according to historical circumstances. Shah Wali-Allah suggests that a prophet is provided with a revelation which stays as close to the natural way of the human being as is possible. However, he also leaves in place any aspect of a previous revelation which is still beneficial to people and adds new revelation which is relevant to the new historical context. He may even have to bring in legislation to supply solutions to accidental events or incidents arising out of particular situations in his life and circumstances.[33] Although Shah Wali-Allah acknowledges that the final revelation given to Muhammad (pbuh) is the closest to *fitra* ever provided to humankind, his analysis of *din* and *shari'a* does provide some flexibility for the individual Muslim to negotiate individual conscience amidst the external dictates of the law.

This possibility is also acknowledged by Hodgson (1974), who argues that the Muslim conscience has expressed itself differently at particular phases of history as they have attempted to respond to their understanding of Allah's purpose for humanity. He suggests that it operates within limits and possibilities imposed by particular situations. [34]

Social conscience

In addition to Eliade's definition of conscience as the inner faculty which determines the moral quality of our thoughts, words and deeds, there is also the view that regards conscience as a social construction. Cicero defines conscience as the internalization of disapproval by others.[35] Although it could be argued that the dominant impact of the formation of the Muslim conscience must come from the nature of the revelation, there can be no doubt that social pressures play a large part. Shah Wali-Allah's analysis of revelation conforms to the orthodox Islamic view that God's will is revealed to communities or a people rather than to individual truth seekers. The individual is perceived as belonging to a community. It is likely that this community (*ummah*) is one which has been formed by the revelation of Allah prior to the final and complete message provided to the last prophet. The Qur'an asserts that God has always revealed his presence and purpose to human communities in order to guide them in the right path. These communities are defined as *ummahs*. Some members of the community have obeyed and some have disobeyed, but all will be judged on their response to the revelation. The Qur'an warns of the fate of those communities which do not listen to the message.[36] The term is used to describe complete communities or peoples who have been chosen to hear God's message. The Qur'an develops the concept of *ummah* into a community of believers united in their common worship of God in the prescribed form as revealed through the Messenger.[37] The final and best *ummah* is the Muslim community. Those who follow the message of the Qur'an, carry out its commandments and worship according to the prescribed rites, live by its code of conduct and obey the last and final Prophet, constitute a model *ummah* (*ummah wusta* or *Ummah Muslimah*). This final *ummah* replaces all the *ummahs* which preceded it. The Qur'an also warns against fragmentation of the *ummah* into sects and commands unity of faith and community.[38] Several Hadith express identification of goodness with conformity to the dictates of Islam and forbid joining schismatic sects or heretical groups.[39] These Hadith identify goodness with faith or loyalty to the community. Consequently the social dimension of conscience is significant within Islam.

At the beginning of Islam's history, membership of the *ummah* supplanted the powerful tribal solidarity of the Arabs as the strongest identity of the individual in relation to society. As already explored, once Islam was established, it carried out major changes in the area of law and social order. Islamic law remodelled and often replaced customary tribal laws.[40] The *ummah* is then a community which can be described as growing out the process of obedience to Islamic law. It is guided by the word of God and the actions of the Prophet, and has a moral mission to create a new social order based on faith and obedience. Muhammad and the early Muslim community are seen as exemplifying this ideal. The ideal has often provided a rationale for political and moral activism based on various interpretations of religious orthodoxy.[41]

Edwards (1967) elaborated on the idea of conscience as internalization of the disapproval of others and stated: 'groups established social customs, or mores, and enforced them; members of these groups who were tempted to violate these mores could almost hear the disapproval of their fellows and hear in their own minds a protesting outcry'.[42] Although the Muslim nations encompass a wide range of interpretations of faith, outward pressures to conform and therefore internalize particular values certainly impact on their social experience. The three areas of significance in this respect would be:

i)   where there are self-defined righteous groups within the wider community who claim that they are the true upholders of Islamic belief and practice. Such groups will call upon the Muslim population to return to strict obedience to the Qur'an and *Sunna* in order to renew the *ummah* and return it to the pristine faith of the Prophet and his companions. These groups will see their position as being the faithful *ummah* within the wider *ummah* which can guide the uncommitted and those who have gone astray.[43]

ii) within the extended family where there will be considerable pressures to conform, based not so much upon Islamic doctrine and practice but more on the concept of honour. The individual member of a family group can disgrace the family through behaviour which does not follow the local mores and customs. This concept of family honour is known as *izzat* within the Indian subcontinent. At this level the Muslim social conscience is formed from a mixture of universal Islamic tenets and local customs which may be given religious sanction and authority.

iii) where Muslims are a minority community and feel threatened by the non-Muslim indigenous culture. In this context the pressures to conform to a perceived orthodoxy are likely to be greater. This will arise out of the community erecting border mechanisms to protect both religion and ethnicity.

The Sufi alternative

Up until this point this article has stressed the formation of Muslim conscience as responding to external sources which are either the dictates of God's revelation in the Qur'an fully fleshed out in the *shari'a* or pressures to conform from the community. However, although the jurists and theologians stressed punishment and reward as the inevitable consequences of God's threats and promises, there were other Muslims who always stressed the love of God.

The Sufis or mystics of Islam have proclaimed the immanence of Allah as well as his transcendence. Fakhri points out that the Hadith indicate that actions are always a product of intention and that everyone will be called to judgement by declaring their original intentions. The locus of intention is the heart (*qalb*).[44] This reality of the *qalb* and the *nafs* (lower self) is important to Sufis and results in a more individual inner awareness of conscience. For a Sufi, one who does not have an inner direct knowledge of God's immanence to complete the outward manifestations of obedience to the law has not yet received full divine illumination. The soul should always be held in readiness to receive the grace of illumination experienced in the realm of the heart. In order to prepare for God's inner revelation it is necessary to clean the impurities of the *nafs*. This inner cleansing is a prelude to the knowledge of God and can be achieved by *dhickr* or constant remembrance of Allah. When the undivided attention is turned to the remembrance of God, the inner world of the Sufi is cleansed and the light of God manifests within the heart.

There have been many methods or *tariqas* followed by Sufis under the guidance of a teacher to achieve their spiritual goal and it is not my intention here to describe them. However, in general, most Sufi orders have taught that there are seven stages which constitute the discipline of the individual Sufi. These stages correspond to ten states or spiritual experiences which come as a gift from the divine.[45] The important point is that for the Sufi, conscience would first manifest as the inner voice of the heart trying to make itself heard over the impurities of the *nafs*. This would call the Sufi to repentance, abstinence and inner renunciation. Once firmly established on the path, conscience would function to remind the Sufi to remain constantly in recollection of the divine. This function of conscience would coincide with the stages of patience and trust in God. At the final stage of satisfaction where the state of union or full absorption of human qualities into the divine is achieved, it is difficult to perceive what role conscience could play as the Sufi now rests in perfect tranquillity in the all-consuming love of God.

There has always been considerable tension between Sufism and orthodox Islam, between the outer and the inner dimensions, between those that emphasize the love of God and those that emphasize fear and judgement. Although the dominant mode of Islam is that of the jurists and religious scholars who focus on the requirements of the *shari'a*, it would not be an accurate portrayal of the faith to leave out the mystical tradition. At certain times in Muslim history and in certain places within the Muslim world its message has been heard and felt by the people, and in many places in the world the love and respect for the saints of Islam still maintains its hold over the religious sensibilities of the Muslim population. In conclusion, then, any analysis of the impact of conscience on the Muslim psyche would have to take into account the influence of the Sufi tradition as well as the more orthodox renderings of Islam. However, it is likely that the manifestations of conscience described in the earlier part of this article will hold sway over the vast majority of Muslims who receive their direction in the faith from peers, family, orthodox religious organizations or the local *imam's* instruction at the mosque.

Notes

1   Majid Fakhry, *Ethical Theories in Islam* (E. J. Brill, Leiden, 1991), p. 1.
2   M. Eliade, *The Encyclopaedia of Religion* (Simon & Schuster, Macmillan, New York, 1995), p. 45.
3   A. Y. Ali (tr.), *The Holy Qur'an,* Sura Al-Imran 3:104, (revised and edited by the Presidency of Islamic Researches, IFTA, *Mushaf Al-Madinah An-Nabawiyah,* King Fahd Holy Qur'an Printing Complex, Saudi Arabia), pp. 171–172.
4   ibid., Al-Imran 3:105, p. 172.
5   ibid., p. 172.
6   It is important to remember that the doctrine of 'Manifest Success' only applies to the majority Sunni Muslims. The Shi'a experience of persecution and martyrdom has resulted in a different direction. Their experience has led them to develop a theology of suffering. In this context I feel that the Shi'as' intense sensibilities and feelings resulting from their history require an independent study of the development of conscience in their tradition of Islam. Consequently, I have not included them in this paper as a separate entity. My discussion of conscience therefore applies in general to all Muslims but does not investigate the unique aspects of Shi'a.
7   ibid., Al-Imran 3:115, p. 175.
8   Eliade, op. cit., p. 45.
9   D. S. Margoulieth, 'Conscience', *Encyclopaedia of Religion and Ethics,* J. Hastings (ed), (T & T Clark, Edinburgh, 1911), p. 47.
10 D. Lodge, 'The Church and Cultural Life', *The Church Now,* J. Cummings, and P. Burns, (eds), (Gill & Macmillan, Dublin, 1980).
11 I. Ramsey, *Christian Ethics and Contemporary Philosophy,* (SCM, London, 1966).
12   But verily over you
         Are appointed angels
         To protect you
         Kind and honourable –

> Writing down your deeds
> They know
> All that ye do.
> As for the Righteous,
> They will be in bliss;
> And the Wicked
> They will be in the Fire (Sura Al-Infitar, 82:10–14).

13 I have not been able to ascertain the Arabic names for these two angels in any text. However, informants have assured me that they are called Kiraman (angel of the right) and Katebeen (angel of the left). My informants are Muslims from the Indian subcontinent and the transliteration of these names is from the Urdu form rather than the Arabic.

14 Sura Qaf 50:17.

15   At length, when death approaches
          One of you. Our angels
          Take his soul, and they
          never fail in their duty (Sura Al-An'am 6:61).

16 G. Hourani, *Reason and Traditions in Islamic Ethics,* (Cambridge University Press, Cambridge, 1985), p. 2.

17 ibid., p. 8.

18 According to Sunni tradition, the Mu'tazila were given their name when their founder, Wasil ibn 'Ata' (80–13/699–749) broke away from Hasan of Basra. They claimed that reason was an equal source of moral truth along with revelation. They were certainly influenced by Hellenistic rationalism. F. Rahman, *Islam,* (University of Chicago Press, Chicago, 1979), pp. 88–89.

19 Hourani, op. cit., p. 8.

20   But is possible
          That ye dislike a thing
          Which is good for you,
          And that ye love a thing
          Which is bad for you.
          But Allah knoweth,
          And ye know not (Sura Al-Baqarah, 2:216, p. 91).

21 Rahman, op.cit., p. 68.

22   We had already, beforehand,
          Taken the covenant of Adam,
          But he forgot: and We found
          On his part no firm resolve (Sura Ta-Ha, 20:115, p. 908).

23 K. Cragg, *Islam and the Muslim,* (Open University, Milton Keynes, 1987), p. 48.

24 Hourani, op. cit., p. 1.

25 Rahman notes that besides the detailed pronouncement on the law of inheritance and the citing of punishments for theft and adultery, there is little that is actually legislative (Rahman, op. cit., p. 69).

26 This represents the use of alternative calendars, the former being the Islamic calendar dating from the *hijra* in 622, and the latter being the Christian calendar.

27 The two most authoritive are Hadith collections by Muhammad ibn Isma'il al-Bukhari (194–256/810–870); Muslim ibn al-Hajjaj (d. 261/875). The other four are by Abu Da'ud (d. 275/888), al-Tirmidhi (d. 279/892), al-Nasa'i (d. 303/916) and Ibn Maja (d. 273/886). Rahman notes that Bukhari's collection is acclaimed as second only to the Qur'an in authority (ibid., pp. 63–64).

28 ibid., p. 64.

29 The Hanifi school is dominant in Western Asia, Lower Egypt, the Indian subcontinent. The Maliki in North and West Africa and Upper Egypt, the Shafi'i in Indonesia, and the Hanbali in Northern and Central Arabia (Rahman, op. cit., p. 83).

30 Joshua Halberstam, 'Supererogation in Jewish Halakhah and Islamic Shari'a', *Studies in Islamic and Judaic Traditions,* W. Brinner, & S. Ricks, (eds.) (Brown Judaic Studies 110, The University of Denver, 1986) p. 93.

31 Rahman, op. cit., p. 84.

32 Marcia Hermansen, (tr.), 'The Conclusive Argument from God - Shah Wali-Allah of Delhi's Hujjat Allah al-Baligha,' *Islamic Philosophy, Theology and Science,* vol.XXV, H. Dauber, and D. Pingree, (eds.) (E. J. Brill, Leiden, 1996), pp. xx–xxii.

33 ibid., p. 290.

34 Marshall, Hodgson, *The Ventures of Islam: Conscience and History in a World Civilisation* (University of Chicago Press, Chicago, 1974), p. 6.

35 Hastings, op. cit., p. 45.

36   To every people was sent
            A Messenger: when their Messenger
            Comes before them, the matter
            Will be judged between them
            With justice, and they
            Will not be wronged (Yunus 10:47, p. 562)

37 R. A. Geaves, *Sectarian Influences within Islam in Britain with special reference to the concepts of Community and ummah,* (Community Religions Monograph, University of Leeds, 1996), p. 13.

38   And verily this *Ummah*
            Of yours is a single *Ummah*
            And I am your Lord
            And Cherisher: therefore
            Fear Me and no other

            But people have cut off
            Their affair of unity
            Between them, into sects:
            Each party rejoices in that
            Which is with itself (Al-Muminun, 23:52-53, p. 988)
39   Fakhry, op. cit., p. 24.
40   Montgomery Watt, *Islam and the Integration of Society*
      (Routledge & Kegan Paul, London, 1961), p. 185ff.
41   Hodgson argues that the *ummah* manifested the Qura'nic
      mandate 'to transform the world itself through action in the
      world', Marshall Hodgson, *The Venture of Islam* vol I,
      (University of Chicago Press, Chicago, 1974), p. 185. Esposito
      supports this view. He argues that based on the Qur'an's
      message to strive to realise God's will in history, the Prophet
      and the first Muslims established the community in Medina
      which then became the inspiration for the mission to spread
      Islam throughout the world. John Esposito, *Islam - the Straight
      Path* (Oxford University Press, New York, 1988), p. 37.
42   P. Edwards, *The Encyclopaedia of Philosophy,* (Collier-
      Macmillan, New York, 1967), p. 189.
43   Such groups will sanction their position from a *sura* of the
      Qur'an which defines *ummah* in a specialised sense. Al-Imran
      3:104 states:
                  Let there arise out of you
                  A band of people
                  Inviting to all that is good,
                  Enjoining what is right,
                  And forbidding what is wrong.
                  They are ones to attain felicity (pp.171-172)
      This seems to suggest that the *ummah* can be applied not only
      to the totality of Muslims but to a righteous group of believers
      who have been selected from the wider community and who are
      charged with the duty of inviting other Muslims to obedience
      (Geaves, op. cit., p. 13).
44   Fakhry, op. cit., p. 25.
45   The *maqawat* are states of spiritual attainment on the Sufi's
      journey which are the result of personal effort, whereas the

ahwal (stages) are a spiritual condition given to the mystic by God. (A. J. Arberry, *Sufism*, (G. Allen & Unwin, London, 1972) p. 75. There are several versions of the stages and states but I have utilised Al-Sarraj's seven states and ten stages which are as follows: (i) conversion, (ii) abstinence (iii) renunciation (iv) poverty (v) patience (vi) trust in God (vii) satisfaction. The stages are: (i) meditation (ii) nearness to God (iii) love (iv) fear (v) hope (vi) longing (vii) intimacy (viii) tranquillity (ix) contemplation (x) certainty (ibid., p. 79).

7

Buddhism and Conscience

George D. Chryssides

To ask for the Buddhist view of conscience is rather like asking for the Church of England's view on something like space travel. Buddhists to whom I have spoken, at least in the west, understand what the concept means, but agree that it simply has no role in Buddhist ethics or religion. Every religion has its own principal concepts, which do not always find ready counterparts within another faith. Making the theme of 'conscience' the focus of a volume such as this creates the risk of skewing an account of a religion where the theme lacks dominance, or is absent entirely. The short but accurate account of the Buddhist view of 'conscience' is that there is none. As Michel Despland, writing in Mircea Eliade's *Encyclopedia of Religion*, notes: 'Hindu and Buddhist philosophies have very articulate and complex theories of consciousness... But the notion of conscience as internal organ is not found outside of Christianity'.[1]

In Hastings' much earlier *Encyclopaedia of Religion and Ethics* (1911), the various contributors of articles on 'Conscience' attribute presumed equivalences of conscience to the religions of the ancient Graeco-Roman, Babylonian and Egyptian empires, and, amongst living religions, to Jews and Muslims only. No mention whatsoever is made of Hinduism or Buddhism.[2]

I could simply end my account of Buddhism and conscience with these few remarks. However, to do so might allow the reader to infer that Buddhism is somehow morally deficient, and that Buddhists lack a fundamental concept which is essential for moral striving and for distinguishing between right and wrong. On this line of reasoning, a Buddhist ought to be the last person with whom one should do business!

There is another line of reasoning that might be tempting. Surely, one might argue, no major religious community could be so lacking in moral awareness as to have no concept of conscience whatsoever. Although Buddhists may not use the word 'conscience', must there not be some equivalent notion which fulfils the same, or at least a very similar role?

The apparent discovery of Christian–Buddhist parallels was a popular nineteenth and early twentieth century pastime amongst western scholars. It was customary to translate the Buddhist term 'Sangha' (the monastic community) as 'Church', or to remark that nirvana (enlightenment) was the Buddhist equivalent of heaven (an assertion which still lingers on in some of the inferior children's books, mainly written by Christians). To some, the 'Ten Precepts' have looked like an equivalent of the Mosaic Ten Commandments.[3]

Clearly there needs to be some common vocabulary amongst different world religions for any mutual understanding to be possible at all, but such supposed parallels are grossly misleading. Although the Sangha can be contrasted with the laity, they are not endowed with special powers, unlike a Christian priesthood or ministry, where, for example, only the priest may celebrate certain sacraments. Unlike the Christian concept of the Church, there is no distinction between a visible and invisible Sangha, nor are there notions of a Sangha militant and triumphant, whatever that would mean. By a similar line of reasoning, nirvana cannot be the 'equivalent' of the Christian heaven. Nirvana is not a 'place' – not even a metaphysical one – and, since Buddhism has typically denied the existence of an immortal unchanging self or soul, there are no individuals who ultimately exist to 'enter' nirvana. I shall comment later on the role of Buddhist Precepts, but it is sufficient to note that they have little more in common with the Ten Commandments than the obvious fact that they are ten in number.

The key question, then, about Buddhism and conscience is not how or why Buddhists come to 'lack' a seemingly fundamental moral sense, nor about what 'equivalents' to conscience can be found within the Buddhist tradition. What we must explore is the fundamental structure of Buddhism's ethical thinking which precludes the notion of conscience finding a niche.

Buddhist and Judaeo-Christian ethics – a comparison

At the risk of begging numerous important questions about religion, morality and conscience, it might, I think, be agreed that Judaism and Christianity are revealed religions in which God has made his will known to humanity through a succession of prophets, and finally – according to the Christian – through his Son.[4]

The prophets and Jesus of Nazareth were much concerned with ensuring that humanity was in no doubt about God's moral requirements. God is essentially 'other' – distinct from and superior to humanity – and hence this distance had to be bridged by such intermediaries. Thus, God gave Moses the Torah (the Law) on Mount Sinai, with promises of rewards for observance, and threats of judgement and punishment for disobedience. According to some Jews and the majority of Christians, the reward for obedience is the continued existence of the self – variously viewed as an immortal soul, distinct from the body, or else as a transformed 'spiritual body'[5] – in a much-desired after-death state, such as the Kingdom of God or the messianic age.

Both religions teach that attainment of their ultimate goal is marred by human sin, a falling short of the standard set by this omnipotent God. Because of humankind's past sins, there will be a judgement which no one will escape, and in which everyone's deserved condemnation for their sinful actions can only be mitigated by renewed obedience to the Law, in the case of Judaism, or – according to the Christian – by faith in the atoning work of Jesus Christ, followed by the sanctifying work of the Holy Spirit, from which appropriate conduct is one important outcome.

Because the Talmud–Torah and the Christian Bible are

works of finite length, and cannot possibly cover every ethical dilemma one is likely to meet, certain devices are needed in order to enable the follower to reach decisions about situations where the appropriate action is unclear. Moreover, because the line of prophecy is only accessible to those within the Jewish and Christian traditions, some account is needed of where this leaves those who live outside Judaeo-Christianity. Are they of necessity morally blind, or have they some other means of access to moral truth? The notion of conscience serves to answer such questions. According to Roman Catholic teaching, for example, conscience is the inner sense which, by employing spiritual aids, such as prayer, the study of Scripture and the Church's tradition, can provide an important, although not infallible, guide to the appropriate solution.[6] Regarding the gentiles, Paul speaks of a 'law ... written on their hearts, their consciences also bearing witness',[7] indicating that they have no excuse for failing to distinguish between right and wrong. As the Westminster *Confession of Faith* puts it: 'God alone is Lord of the conscience, and hath left it free from the doctrines and commandments of men which are in anything contrary to his word, or beside it, in matters of faith or worship'.[8]

It is worth mentioning, too, that although conscience is something possessed by the individual, the dictates of conscience are not subjective. Although conscience is the 'voice within', it by no means follows that rightness and wrongness are matters of individual feeling or decision. The truth is 'out there', and conscience's function is to determine what is objectively true and false in moral matters.

Buddhist ethics and the law of karma

The Buddhist position on ethics contrasts with this outline of Judaeo-Christianity in almost every respect. Buddhism is not a revealed or a prophetic religion: it does not hold that a god or gods either create or mediate a moral law. It is not quite accurate to describe Buddhism as an 'atheistic religion' – a characterization that one so often finds. Buddhism quite readily acknowledges the existence of gods, but relegates them to one realm of impermanent existence among several. Someone might be reborn as a god – a pleasant enough existence while it lasts – but that god will subsequently be reborn into some other realm of existence, for example as an animal, a human or in one of the hells. While the gods can offer pragmatic benefits to those who pray to them, they have no role in affording any kind of moral guidance or spiritual progress to those who approach them. The gods, in short, are not moral lawgivers.

Just as there is no permanent underlying substance which supports the universe's existence, such as a creator-sustainer God, so there is no inner substantiality in anything in the universe, including human beings. Human beings, in common with everything else, are subject to *anatta,* which literally means 'no soul'. According to the Buddhist, everything is *anicca* – impermanent – subject to constant change, without there being anything substantial that exists as the subject of change. What we take to be the human self is just a bundle of sensations, known as the five *khandhas* ('aggregates'): form, feeling, thought, choice, and consciousness.[9]

It might be asked whether it might be the Buddha who occupies the role of lawgiver in place of a supreme deity. The incorrectness of this suggestion can readily be seen from the story of the Buddha's enlightenment. According to Buddhist myth, Siddhartha Gautama, the Buddha-to-be, having renounced the extremes of princely wealth and the fearsome austerities of the ascetic life, sat under a pipal tree, in Bodh Gaya in North India, until he attained the supreme goal of nirvana. The experience of enlightenment, which came to him on the seventh day of his meditation, came in four distinct stages. First, he gained knowledge of his previous lives. (It is said that there were 530 of these, and they are recorded in Buddhist tales known as the *Jatakas.)* Second, he 'acquired the supreme heavenly eye', through which he realized that the process of birth and rebirth depended on one's deeds, and not – as the Indians of the Buddha's time popularly believed – on the fulfilment of one's caste obligations, or on placating the gods through the Vedic sacrificial system.

Third, the Buddha perceived 'the real and essential nature of the world'. This is typically expressed as a set of twelve links in a chain, and is known as the doctrine of 'dependent origination' *(nidanas)*. According to this teaching, each of the following links, unless it is broken, gives rise to the next: ignorance – karma-formations – consciousness – name and form – six sense fields – contact – feeling – craving – grasping – becoming – birth – decay and death.[10] (I shall explain the meaning and significance of this list later.)

In the fourth and final stage, the Buddha gained the supreme enlightenment he had been seeking, in which he experienced inner peace and saw things 'as they really are'. His account of the true nature of the world is expressed in his first sermon after becoming enlightened, in which the Buddha taught the famous Four Noble Truths and the Eightfold Path – teachings which are often held to sum up the essence of Buddhism. The Four Noble Truths are:

The existence of unsatisfactoriness *(dukkha)*
The cause of unsatisfactoriness *(samudaya)*
The elimination of unsatisfactoriness *(nirodha)*
The path to the elimination of unsatisfactoriness *(magga)*.

The Eightfold Path is thus the fourth Noble Truth, and consists of:

Perfect view
Perfect aspiration
Perfect speech
Perfect conduct
Perfect livelihood
Perfect effort
Perfect meditation
Perfect 'absorption'.[11]

Buddhists typically divide this list into three unequal sections: wisdom (points 1 and 2), morality (points 3, 4 and 5) and meditation (points 6, 7 and 8).

'Perfect view' (seeing things as they really are) involves recognizing the unsatisfactory nature of existence. According to Buddhist teaching, the universe is subject to three 'marks of existence': *anatta* ('no self' or insubstantiality), *anicca* (impermanence) and *dukkha* (unsatisfactoriness). A conative element is contained in the second point ('aspiration').

Attaining enlightenment is not simply recognition, but involves spiritual striving. This in turn entails the three points that follow on the list – perfect speech, conduct and livelihood – and these must interact with the meditative life which classical Theravada Buddhism (amongst others) enjoins.

The point that emerges is that one should not accept the Buddha's teaching simply on his authority, but rather should come to see the world for oneself in the same way as the Buddha did. In such a state one apprehends the way in which the law of karma operates, and the types of action which are instrumental in bringing about release from the cycle of birth and rebirth. (Buddhists, in common with Hindus and Sikhs, call this cycle *samsara.*) What is right, then, is what is conducive to aspiring towards nirvana; what is wrong is defined as that which is harmful towards spiritual progress. In fact, Buddhists are less inclined to talk in terms of 'right and wrong' than to use the terms 'skilful' and 'unskilful' about actions. In Buddhist thinking, a good action is rather like the action, say, of an archer aiming the arrow towards a target. Just as the skilled archer hits the bull's eye, so the morally 'skilful' person is successfully aiming towards the mark.

It is not sufficient merely to agree that the Buddha truly defined the way reality is. The first point of the Eightfold Path is 'right view' not 'right views', a confusion often incurred by western commentators who are heavily influenced by Christianity's relentless quest for 'sound doctrine'. (My use of the expression 'perfect view' in preference to 'right view' is intended to obviate this error.) There is all the difference in the world between my believing someone who says that there is a wonderful view outside my window, and my looking out of the window to see it for myself. Similarly, an enlightened person is not someone with a mental filing cabinet full of completely true beliefs, but someone who actually sees the world as subject to the three marks of existence, recognizes how the law of karma operates, and thus knows directly which actions are 'skilful' and which are 'unskilful'.

All this points to a fundamental distinction between Buddhist and Judaeo-Christian ethics. While the latter is *prescriptive* (that is to say, it is cast in the form of numerous imperatives which must be followed), Buddhist ethics is *descriptive.* The law of karma dictates that actions which are in accordance with the *Dharma* (the Buddha's teaching) will bring about good fortune, and that evil actions bring about misfortune and suffering, if not in this life, at least in some future existence. There is no god who intervenes to ensure that one receives one's just deserts, or who has set a day of judgement on which all humankind will have to account for their lives.[12] The law of karma works like a law of nature: indeed, Buddhists often make a comparison between the law of karma and natural laws such as the law of gravity. Just as letting go of an object in mid-air will have the inevitable consequence of that object's falling to the floor, so the effects of one's deeds come to inevitable fruition in due course.[13]

The descriptive rather than prescriptive nature of Buddhist ethics enables a somewhat relaxed attitude to the laity's observance of the Precepts. It is important to note that Buddhists typically use the term 'precept' rather than 'commandment', for two reasons. First, as we have noted, the Buddhist way of life does not emanate from a divine lawgiver. Second, a precept, being akin to a vow, is something that the aspirant assumes when he or she is ready for it. Thus, some Buddhists may not feel ready to give up alcohol, and are therefore under no compulsion to do so. They can do so when they are ready, and, if they find themselves attending a ceremony in which the precepts are mentioned, they will remain silent when the precept that proscribes intoxicants is recited. In the meantime, of course, drinking alcohol will generate its own karma, for which the price must be paid in due course.

Lest the Buddhist attitude to morality be misunderstood, it should be emphasised that what may seem a casual attitude to the precepts does not entail that anything is tolerated within a Buddhist society. Where actions are harmful to the social order, such as theft or murder, penalties are prescribed and enforced. (Recent news reports have made it plain how little sympathy is afforded to drug smugglers in Thailand, for example.) The Sangha itself, which is a society in its own right, has to have strict and enforceable rules, and joining the Sangha presumes that all the monastic precepts have been taken on. Monks are subjected to a monthly ceremony of confession (on *uposatha* – 'Observance Day'), in which they are expected, in the presence of the other monks, to admit to any infringements of the rules of the *vinaya* (monastic precepts), and serious infringement of such rules *(sangha-beda),* such as fornication, is a grave offence, which merits expulsion.

To recapitulate: the points that emerge from the myth of the Buddha's enlightenment are these. First, enlightenment entails seeing and knowing how the law of karma operates. Second, karmic consequences depend on one's deeds. Third, an enlightened being sees things truly as they are – a state which encompasses the previous two points.

The doctrine of 'dependent origination' demonstrates the way in which these points are interconnected. The theory is so called because it purports to show how the arising of certain phenomena is dependent on the presence of the relevant antecedent state. Let us take one example of how one link in this chain gives rise to the next. Ignorance is held to give rise to 'karma formations'. In other words, if I lack 'perfect view' ('seeing things as they really are', which is the characteristic feature of enlightenment), the law of karma will continue to operate, and I will reap the effects of my past deeds. This will entail the arising of another conscious being – my next rebirth. And so the chain continues in motion. Unless the chain is broken, the law of karma will roll on relentlessly in this fashion.

The doctrine of the *nidanas* is colloquially referred to as 'the law of cause and effect'. This is somewhat misleading. In the physical sciences, a cause inevitably gives rise to its effect. Friction inevitably causes heat, for example. The chain of dependent origination is different, because it is possible to break the links in the chain. It is possible, although difficult, to dispel ignorance, as Gautama successfully accomplished. When this occurs, the next stage in the chain will not be acti-vated: when the Buddha finally reached his *parinirvana* (demise after attaining enlightenment), no further rebirths occurred. One can try to break the chain by eliminating selfish desire (*tanha*); when this is successfully achieved, no grasp-ing will follow, and hence no becoming, no birth, decay and death.

We might therefore describe the Buddhist interest in morality as 'forward looking' rather than 'past looking'. Buddhism is not so much interested in the origins of morality so much as its goal. The Buddha is said to have used an analogy which illustrates this point. A man lies dying from a wound caused by a poisoned arrow. Some of the onlookers debate amongst themselves who fired the arrow – whether he was tall or short, dark or fair, and so on. What is more important, the Buddha taught, is to pull the arrow out, thus enabling the poison (the vices which hold one back from enlightenment) to be removed.[14]

What is important to the Buddhist, therefore, is not to ask questions about the origin of morality, or how we became subject to the state of selfish desire which is characteristic of *dukkha*. Spiritual progress will not be gained by speculating about the origins of the universe or of morality, but rather by recognizing the effects of one's deeds and how they can be skilful or unskilful in bringing the aspirant towards nirvana. Questions about whether actions are right because God commanded them or vice versa, and how members of the human race are placed spiritually if they have not been party to divine commandments are therefore non-questions. The Buddhist simply has no need for a theory of conscience as an attempt to explain how certain sectors of humanity are placed if they have not heard God's decrees.

There is thus no counterpart in Buddhism to 'doing God's will'. One cannot 'do the Buddha's will'. The Buddha has 'thus gone', according to the Theravada tradition: he is 'beyond recall' (that is to say, it is impossible to speculate on the nature of his existence after *parinirvana)*, and hence is neither pleased nor displeased at human deeds. At best the Buddha is an example to follow. As the classical text, the *Dhammapada* puts it, 'It is you who must make the effort. The Great of the past only show the way.'[15]

It might be suggested that a possible parallel to the Christian theory of conscience lies in the fact that the Buddha's teach-ings, according to the Buddhist, are not to be accepted simply on authority. The Buddha is said to have invited seekers to check out his teachings against their own experience, and only to accept them if their experience confirmed what he taught. On one occasion, the Buddha is reported to have instructed a seeker to go back and follow his own (non-Buddhist) religion, to make what progress he could there.

Accounts such as these may be thought to suggest that the Buddha was somehow appealing to the individual consciences of men and women, even allowing them conscientiously to disagree with his philosophy. But to draw such a conclusion would be to misunderstand the Buddha's message. The Buddha was not recommending some kind of subjective individualism or relativism. On the contrary, the Buddha, as an enlightened being, saw things as they really were. If anyone should think, for example, that the world was not subject to *anatta, anicca* and *dukkha,* then that person would be deluded and thereby be seriously hindered from making spiritual progress. In teaching 'perfect view' as the first point of the Eightfold Path, the Buddha could hardly have meant that any view was equally acceptable.

The correct explanation of the Buddha's invitation to verify his teachings is that, if he did indeed see things as they really were, then anyone else who used the appropriate means of verification would reach the same conclusion. A universal truth can be seen by anyone who looks aright. To use an analogy: if I say that it is raining and you do not believe me, I might reasonably ask you to adopt the same vantage point as myself and look out of the window. My invitation to verification in no way means that I would expect, let alone accept, a variety of opinions regarding the weather. What I expect is that you will see a part of reality in the same way as I do, by direct experience, rather than merely taking my word for it. There is thus no subjectivity about the state of enlightenment: what the Buddha taught was a set of objective universal laws about the way in which the universe operates.

When the Buddha recommended that the seeker should follow his own religion, he was not implying that other religions were equally true, but merely that skilful means could sometimes entail making better progress on a lesser path rather than making very poor progress on a path for which one is not yet ready. In a similar way, being a poor mountaineer, I would be ill-advised to tackle the ascent of Everest; hill walking, on the other hand, is well within my capability, and might be good preliminary training if Everest is my ultimate goal. Similarly, while Buddhists may appear to accept that it could be 'skilful' to practise a non-Buddhist religion, this is only a temporary measure, which will be superseded at some future time, perhaps even in some future life, when one is properly ready to assume the Buddhist path.

One further, final point of contrast is worth mentioning. Whereas Judaeo-Christian ethics (and indeed most of western ethics) tends to focus on actions, Buddhist ethics is essentially about one's intentions and one's state of consciousness. The issue of vegetarianism will illustrate this well. Those who are familiar with western ways of moral reasoning, whether Christian or not, may reason as follows. Since cruelty to animals is reprehensible, then surely one should have qualms of conscience about eating meat. Having become persuaded of the case for vegetarianism, someone might then consider how far one takes this principle of respect for all living beings. Is it sufficient, for example, simply to avoid foods that show obvious signs of being derived from animal flesh, or should one meticulously consider whether there are traces of animal products in the ingredients, such as animal rennet in cheese, or animal fat in certain biscuits? Some vegetarians have gone further and suggested that it is unreasonable simply to stop using animal products for eating. Can one in all conscience wear leather shoes, for instance? At least one vegetarian organization has produced literature indicating where animal products are used in household goods such as glues, or where products have been tested on animals.[16]

The Buddhist approach to animal suffering is very different, and, although some writers have argued the case that Buddhism entails vegetarianism, this claim is actually quite wide of the mark, and really is the result of the application of western moral reasoning to a religion that does not seek to accommodate it.[17] The Buddhist stance on the treatment of animals is based on two important considerations: first, non-violence, which entails abstaining from killing or injuring any living being; second, purifying one's mind by cultivating non-attachment, thus fostering the elimination of selfish desire *(tanha)*.

Although non-violence is one of Buddhism's principal precepts, the Buddhist monk has no objection to the consumption of meat or fish products. Indeed, if a lay person places such items in his alms bowl, he is obliged to accept them. To do otherwise would be to become attached to what one eats, and cultivation of the purity of mind involves rising above this. What is obligatory for the monk is to ensure that he has no direct role in the killing itself. A monk may not specify to a lay follower, if invited to a meal, that he would like a particular meat dish – or indeed any other kind of food. To express a preference would be to show attachment and deliberately to order meat would be regarded as tantamount to commissioning an animal's slaughter. If he 'hears, sees or suspects' that an animal has been specially killed on his behalf, then – and only then – does he have an obligation to refuse.[18]

Those who are accustomed to western ways of thinking about ethics typically find problems with the Buddhist monk's position, since they stand in marked contrast to western presuppositions about moral reasoning. For example, in the West we tend to think, encouraged by writers such as Kant,[19] that moral principles must be universalizable: if it is wrong for me to do something, it is wrong for everyone else in similar circumstances. We tend to demand consistency in the application of moral principles: if I claim to be vegetarian, I ought to be committed to avoiding all products with any trace of animal produce. We tend to assume that, if something is wrong, we ought to discourage others from doing it: when persuasion fails, critics of fast-food stores try picketing, and anti-abortionists attempt to secure legislation. It is a common assumption, too, that if we disapprove of something we should not benefit from it. (This is the underlying principle behind ethical investment, for example, since selling shares in unethical firms in no way hampers their operation.)

It is important to see how the Buddhist approach to ethics contrasts with this. Buddhism regards spiritual progress as a gradual one. Since purifying one's mind is something which is practically impossible outside the monastic life, joining the Sangha is generally viewed – by Theravada Buddhists at any rate – as essential for the ultimate attainment of nirvana. Although the Sangha requires for its continued existence a laity who have to live amidst the 'defilements' of everyday life, they may well not currently be in a position to assume the robe, but may do so either later on in their lives, or else in some future rebirth. What is important to the monk is to rise above the secular life in which violence to living beings is so difficult to avoid. The following short verse from the Buddhist text *The Dhammapada* is often used as a summary of the Buddhist position on ethics:

> Do not what is evil. Do what is good. Keep your mind pure. This is the teaching of Buddha.[20]

At first appearance, the verse may seem singularly uninformative. However, the third sentence in particular sums up very appropriately the way in which the monastic community treats the issue of right and wrong. What is important is to be free from defilements and attachments. As one Buddhist monk pointed out to me, it would not be sufficient for a Buddhist who wanted to make spiritual progress to abandon meat-eating in favour of artificial meats, such as texturized soya or imitation meats which one often finds on the menu in Chinese restaurants. To desire such foods indicates that one still possesses an attachment to meat, which is not conducive to the elimination of *tanha*.

Two case studies: Zen and Soka Gakkai

Thus far I have either generalised about Buddhist ethics, or focused on the traditional Theravada standpoint. It might therefore be useful to examine two other forms of Buddhism in the Mahayana tradition which, at least on first appearance, might seem to come close to Judaeo-Christian ideas of conscience. The examples I have chosen are, first, Zen, and, second, Soka Gakkai, a form of Nichiren Buddhism.

Zen

Zen originated in China in the sixth century BCE, having been brought there by Bodhidharma – at least according to legend. Zen combined many of the basic elements of Indian Buddhism with classical Taoist philosophy. Zen is characteristically summarized in a four line verse, possibly composed by Rinzai

(1141–1215), the famous Zen master, which runs as follows:

> A special transmission outside the scriptures;
> No dependence upon words or letters;
> Direct pointing into one's heart;
> Seeing into one's own nature, and becoming a Buddha.

According to Zen, one's buddha-nature is within oneself. While traditional Theravada Buddhists might look to the Buddha as an example to follow, Zen typically teaches that using the historical Buddha as an exemplar could be positively harmful to spiritual progress. As Rinzai's four line summary implies, my own Buddha-nature in late twentieth century Britain might well be considerably different from that of Siddhartha Gautama's enlightened state in North India in the sixth century BCE.

An oft-quoted Zen parable tells of a young novice monk whom his spiritual master once found in the meditation hall, seated in the lotus position, meditating. 'What do you think you are doing?' asked the master. 'I am trying to become a buddha,' the novice replied. Thereupon the master took a brick and started to polish it. The novice, puzzled, asked what the master was doing. 'I am trying to make a mirror,' the latter replied. 'But you cannot make a mirror out of a brick!' protested the novice. 'And neither can you become a buddha simply by meditating cross-legged on the floor,' the master replied. The point of the anecdote is that the novice thought that he could attain enlightenment by means of a set of practices that someone else had devised. Buddhahood, on the contrary, must come from 'within', not 'without'.[21]

This point serves to explain the practice of using *koans,* which is found in the Rinzai Zen school. The *koan* is an enigmatic question which has no logical answer, such as, 'What is the sound of one hand clapping?' A logical answer, such as pointing out that clapping requires two hands, is unacceptable; the novice must search his or her inner being for some intuitive answer that emanates from this buddha-nature within. Acceptable responses have included decisively thrusting one's hand forward, shouting in a frenzied way, or uttering some seemingly irrelevant expression like 'the cherry tree in the back garden'. (Obviously, if one were simply to borrow such answers and take them to a Zen master, this would be unacceptable, since they would not emanate from one's own buddha-nature, but be mere attempts to copy those of others. Zen masters are reputed to be well trained and able to identify any such deception.)

The idea that one should bring out and develop one's own inner buddha-nature became popular in the USA in the late 1950s and early 1960s, when numerous beatniks and hippies took up Zen Buddhism – at least as they construed it. Those who have read the novels of Jack Kerouac will recognise the stereotype of the Zen Buddhist as someone who does as he or she pleases, letting spontaneity take precedence over the traditional rules of society. Thus, in Kerouac's *The Dharma Bums,* the principal characters simply loaf around, rejecting any ideas of gainful employment, hitching illicit lifts on freight trains, getting drunk on cheap wine, and engaging in free sex with other *'bodhisattvas',* as they call themselves.[22]

This form of Zen was subsequently known as 'Beat Zen', and popularized by such writers as Jack Kerouac, Allen Ginsburg and Alan Watts, but it is generally repudiated by exponents of traditional Zen, or 'Square Zen', as it has sometimes been called. Traditional Zen involves combining what are often fairly precise rules with one's individual spontaneity and creativity. Anyone who has read works like *Zen in the Art of Archery* or *Zen in the Art of Flower Arrangement* will understand that those who have learnt such arts in the context of Zen have had to master an array of traditional methods of practising skills.[23] Notions like individuality and spontaneity by no means imply that 'anything goes'. When Eugen Herrigel, the archery student, interposed his own innovation in archery technique, his Zen teacher instantly dismissed him as a pupil, and it was only with great difficulty that he became reinstated.[24]

The problem about equating the buddha-nature with conscience is that Beat Zen appears to endorse subjectivism, even moral anarchy, where anything goes so long as one is pleasing oneself to best advantage. Although conscience is deemed to be 'within', following conscience is not to be equated with subjectivism. On the contrary, conscience is held to be the mechanism whereby the believer attunes himself or herself with the will of God. While Christianity has attached considerable importance to the idea of acting 'conscientiously', by which it has even meant acting against the tradition's teaching if the believers hold that they 'can do no other', conscience is not judged to be infallible, and can sometimes be mistaken in purporting to mediate the voice of God. The possibility that conscience can err is no doubt one of the main reasons why the Roman Catholic Church officially teaches that conscience requires spiritual education.

'Square Zen' may therefore seem to have more in common with the Christian tradition, since the traditional Zen master will cause his or her pupils to undertake appropriate spiritual exercises, such as *zazen* meditation and (in the Rinzai tradition) *koan* practice. Inner promptings are to be combined with and related to traditional rules, in order to achieve the appropriate outcome. However, there are important differences which should not be ignored. First, the recognition of enlightenment in Zen is not confined to ethical decision making. The experience of *satori* (the Zen word for enlightenment) relates to the whole of life, and is about experiencing all of the world in an enhanced way. As the oft-quoted passage in *Zen and the Art of Motorcycle Maintenance* puts it: 'The Buddha, the Godhead, resides quite as comfortably in the circuits of a digital computer or the gears of a cycle transmission as he does at the top of a mountain or in the petals of a flower'.[25]

Second, the thrust of Zen is towards divergence rather than convergence. If Zen novices differ on how to answer the same *koan*, such divergence could be a signal of their enlightenment. By contrast, if two Christians have a conscientious disagreement on a matter of ethics, they cannot both be right. Pro-abortionists and anti-abortionists can claim to hold their respective positions and act accordingly as a matter of conscience, but if conscience is the voice of God within, presumably God does not speak with two contradictory voices to different Christians. The inner buddha-nature, which is so crucial to the practitioner of Zen, therefore fails to offer a true counterpart to the concept of conscience.

Soka Gakkai

The second case study I have chosen is the Soka Gakkai, a form of Mahayana Buddhism in the Nichiren tradition, which took its rise in the eleventh century BCE in Japan. 'Soka Gakkai' literally means 'value creation', and, when I have asked members of Soka Gakkai International about a possible place for a notion of 'conscience' they have invariably said that, although conscience itself is not a term which they use, nevertheless their notion of 'value creation' comes nearest to it. Indeed, the only explicit Buddhist reference to conscience that I succeeded in finding is by its leader Diasaku Ikeda, in a volume entitled *Choose Life: A Dialogue*, which is a compilation of conversations between Ikeda and the celebrated historian Arnold Toynbee.[26]

Until 1991, the Soka Gakkai were known as the Nichiren Shoshu or NSUK (Nichiren Shoshu of the United Kingdom) in Britain, and were popularly known for their practice of chanting the famous mantra *'nam myoho renge kyo'*. The mantra derives from the title of the movement's principal religious text, *The Lotus Sutra,* which Nichiren (1222–1282), the founder–leader of the Nichiren Buddhist schools, declared to be the definitive Buddhist Scripture, which encapsulated the entirety of Buddhist doctrine. Soka Gokkai Buddhists therefore chant the mantra, and key chapters of the Lotus Sutra, in front of a small wooden shrine known as the *gohonzon.*

'Nam myoho renge kyo' (which literally means 'Homage to the lotus of the true law') is simultaneously a means of paying respect to the Lotus Sutra and a means to gaining pragmatic as well as spiritual benefits. Thus, a Soka Gakkai follower can chant for benefits which are as seemingly materialistic as passing an exam, acquiring a new car, or finding a partner of the opposite sex. In many respects, the practice of chanting bears affinities to a Christian's intercessory prayer: literal results are not guaranteed, but at least if the practitioner does not gain the desired material boon, he or she will acquire the state of mind which is capable of accepting one's lot without it. One important difference, of course, is that the chanting of *'nam myoho renge kyo'* is not addressed to any supernatural being or beings.

Soka Gakkai Buddhists share with other Buddhists a firm belief in karma. My present condition is due to deeds committed in this life and in previous ones. I am therefore responsible for my own situation, and should not hide behind excuses. Just as I am responsible for my past and my present, I am also responsible for my future. Traditional Buddhism has developed a cosmology which postulates several realms of existence into which subsequent rebirths are possible. Soka Gakkai Buddhism postulates ten such realms, but 'demythologizes' them by viewing them as 'basic inner states of being which we all experience from moment to moment': hell, hunger, animality, anger, tranquillity, rapture, learning, realization, bodhisattva and buddhahood.[27] By the choices I make I can determine whether I am essentially in the world of the hells, the hungry spirits, animality, and so on, or whether I am essentially a bodhisattva or a buddha.

This is where the notion of 'value creation' enters the practice of Soka Gakkai Buddhism. Depending on my state of being, I can decide whether to act either out of greed or hatred, or out of love and conscience. Love and conscience, however, are not ends in themselves, for, as Ikeda points out, many of history's atrocities have been committed in the name of both: 'Only when love is directed towards all humankind and all other forms of life on earth and only when conscience is based on an unbounded respect for the dignity of life, will both manifest good aspects.'[28]

Conscience must therefore be directed towards bringing about what is of ultimate value to human beings generally: in particular, the Soka Gakkai desire to bring about world peace, and a significant amount of their chanting is directed to this end. Using the chant ought not therefore to be simply a means of enabling me to achieve my own selfish desires. Soka Gakkai Buddhism is not egoism or hedonism, or even subjectivism. There are things that are potentially of value outside me, but it is through exploring my own inner buddha-nature that I can come to see what is truly of value, and what is not.

There may appear to be certain similarities between 'value creation' (which Ikeda relates to conscience) and Christian ideas of conscience here. There is the teaching of Buddha, which is encapsulated in a portion of Scripture which does not in itself provide particularly lucid and unambiguous guidance for life, apart from the power of the chant. In order to determine what is appropriate behaviour, one has to turn inward to one's buddha-nature, which one may be tempted to equate with conscience, and which clarifies one's moral principles, applying them to uncertain situations, providing definite judgements regarding concrete acts, and thus enabling the practitioner to act responsibly. Contacting one's buddha-nature, like listening to the voice of conscience, is carried out within the context of religious practice, such as the *gongyo* ceremony in which followers chant *'nam myoho renge kyo'*.

While there may appear to be some similarities, it is important not to overlook some very clear differences here between one's buddha-nature and the voice of conscience. According to the Judaeo-Christian tradition, conscience is the means by which God, who is transcendent, and who stands – at least in some sense – 'above' or 'outside' the human self, communicates his will. This cannot, however, be the Buddhist view of the relationship between the self and the Buddha. As we have noted, there is no self, and, if there is no self, there is nothing ultimately to distinguish me from the Buddha. As Richard Causton, the late British Soka Gakkai leader has put it, there is an equality between myself and the Buddha, for the buddha-nature is none other than me. Further, since (as we have noted) Soka Gakkai Buddhists firmly believe in the law of karma, what I discover within my buddha-nature is not a clarification of some legal system which has been laid down by a transcendent God, like the law which was given on Mount Sinai, but a 'descriptive law' about cause and effect, a law that enables me to see the karmic consequences of my behaviour, and to live my life accordingly.

Some conclusions

My analysis of how Buddhist ethics works demonstrates why the concept of conscience rests uneasily with the Buddhist way of thinking. Yet it is important to note that it by no means follows that Buddhists are less concerned about ethics than Jews, Christians or secular humanists. As with their western counterparts, ethics is important both for the maintenance of social order and for making spiritual progress.

It does not follow, either, that Buddhism has no place for remorse or repentance. Indeed, there are many Buddhist tales of notorious villains who have thought better of their ways and turned their lives around. One particularly well-known tale is that of Milarepa, who sought revenge on his family, following a dispute about his inheritance. The story goes that Milarepa learnt black magic from a Tibetan sorcerer, and subsequently used his occult powers to kill scores of his relatives. Later he became racked with remorse, and sought refuge with a Buddhist teacher called Marpa, who prescribed stringent physical and spiritual exercises to ensure Milarepa's commitment. As a result of his penitence and his total obedience to his teacher, Milarepa attained buddhahood, and thus avoided inheriting a large amount of evil karma, which would have consigned him to spending aeons in subsequent existences in the Buddhist hells.[29]

Like Jews, Christians and Muslims, Buddhists too insist that there are sanctions for good and bad behaviour. Such sanctions are more likely to be internal rather than external, although not exclusively so. Purifying the mind of the three cardinal evils – hatred, greed and delusion (ignorance) – is the consequence of developing loving-kindness *(metta)* towards all beings. 'Eleven blessings' are said to follow the cultivation of this virtue:

> One sleeps in comfort.
> One awakens in comfort.
> One doesn't have bad dreams.
> One is dear to human beings.
> One is dear to non-human beings.
> *Devas*[30] guard one.
> Fire, poison and weapons do not affect one.
> One's mind is easily concentrated.
> One's mien is serene.
> One dies unconfused.
> If one penetrates no higher, one will be reborn in the world of Brahma.[31]

The benefits, it will be noticed, are physical, mental and spiritual.

In common, then, with the prophetic religions, Buddhism entails adherence to a rigorous and detailed set of moral values. A moral life is conducive to peace of mind and spiritual advancement, and there is scope for confession of faults, remorse and penitence. Morality is accompanied by appropriate sanctions.

Buddhist ethics, however, has no room for the concept of conscience, as it is understood by Christians, because it is not a revealed religion. There is no God who gives his decrees to his followers, and there are no permanent enduring selves to be the recipients of any such revelations. It would be incoherent to postulate the existence of any internal faculty which sought to attune one's moral sense with that of some supreme lawgiver. Buddhist ethics is about consciousness, not about conscience, and the Buddhist's spiritual path depends on awareness of the way in which the universe operates, and how to act skilfully to develop one's consciousness in such a way as to progress towards the supreme goal of nirvana.

Notes

1   M. Despland, 'Conscience'; in M. Eliade, *The Encyclopedia of Religion* (Simon & Schuster, New York, 1995), pp. 45–52.
2   J. Hastings, *Encyclopaedia of Religion and Ethics* (T. & T. Clark, Edinburgh, 1911).
3   P. Almond, *The British Discovery of Buddhism* (Cambridge University Press, Cambridge, 1988), p. 107.
4   Heb. 1.1.
5   1 Cor. 15.44.
6   *Catechism of the Catholic Church* (Geoffrey Chapman, London, 1994), para. 1785.
7   Rom. 2.15.
8   *The Confession of Faith,* agreed upon by The Assembly of Divines at Westminster (William Blackwood & Sons, Edinburgh, 1647, 1969), ch. XX, ii.
9   Some westerners, with some justification, have seen similarities between the Buddhist view of the self and David Hume's theory of personal identity, in which he viewed the self as a fiction and nothing more than an arbitrary bundle of 'impressions'. For a discussion of how there can be persons without selves, see

S. Collins, *Selfless Persons* (Cambridge University Press, Cambridge, 1982).

10 E. Conze, *Buddhist Scriptures* (Penguin, Harmondsworth, 1957), p. 187. R. C. Zaehner, (ed.), *The Hutchinson Encyclopedia of Living Faiths* (Helicon, Oxford, 1988), p. 279.

11 For an explanation of the precise meaning of these points, see F. L. Woodward, tr., *Some Sayings of the Buddha according to the Pali Canon*. (The Buddhist Society, London, 1973).

12 Acts 17.31.

13 R. Causton, *Nichiren Shoshu Buddhism: an Introduction* (Rider, London, 1988), pp. 165–195. J. Cowan, (ed.), *The Buddhism of the Sun* (NSUK, Richmond, 1982), pp. 73–75.

14 *Majjihima-Nikaya,* I, ch. 63; in Woodward, op. cit., pp. 202–205.

15 J. Mascaro, tr., *The Dhammapada* (Penguin, Harmondsworth, 1977), verse 276.

16 R. Farhall, K. McCormack, and A. Rofe, *Animal Free Shopper* (The Vegan Society, St Leonards-on-Sea, 1993).

17 P. Kapleau, *A Buddhist Case for Vegetarianism* (Rider, London, 1983). George Chryssides, 'Buddhism goes west'; *World Faiths Insight*, New Series 20, October 1988, pp. 37–45.

18 George Chryssides, *The Path of Buddhism* (Saint Andrew Press, Edinburgh, 1988), p. 50.

19 Immanuel Kant, *Groundwork of the Metaphysic of Morals* (1979) reprinted as H. J. Paton, *The Moral Law* (Hutchinson, London, 1964).

20 *The Dhammapada,* verse 183.

21 A. Watts, *The Way of Zen* (Penguin, Harmondsworth, 1957, 1976), pp. 116–117.

22 J. Kerouac, *On the Road* (Penguin, Harmondsworth, 1957). J. Kerouac, *The Dharma Bums* (Viking, New York, 1957). 'Bodhisattva' means variously 'a buddha-to-be' (in the Theravada tradition) or one who has attained enlightenment but chooses to incarnate again in order to help other living beings.

23 E. Herrigel, *Zen in the Art of Archery* (Routledge & Kegan Paul, London, 1953, 1979). G. L. Herrigel, *Zen in the Art of Flower Arrangement* (Routledge & Kegan Paul, London, 1958, 1979).

24 E. Herrigel, op. cit., p. 71.

25 R. Pirsig, *Zen and the Art of Motorcycle Maintenance* (Corgi, London, 1974), p. 18.

26 A. Toynbee and D. Ikeda, *Choose Life: A Dialogue* (Oxford University Press, London, 1976).

27 Causton, op. cit., p. 36.

28 Toynbee and Ikeda, op. cit., p. 329.
29 Lobsang P. Lhalungpa, *The Life of Milarepa* (Granada, London, 1979).
30 i.e. gods.
31 H. Saddhatissa, *Buddhist Ethics: Essence of Buddhism* (George Allen & Unwin, London, 1970), p. 97.